Journal Excerpts *from the* Ring *of* Fire

BARBARA WOLF

authorHOUSE®

AuthorHouse™ LLC
1663 Liberty Drive
Bloomington, IN 47403
www.authorhouse.com
Phone: 1-800-839-8640

Published by AuthorHouse 07/24/2014

ISBN: 978-1-4969-2739-2 (sc)
ISBN: 978-1-4969-2740-8 (hc)
ISBN: 978-1-4969-2738-5 (e)

Library of Congress Control Number: 2014913292

CONTENTS

This book is dedicated to my husband Jack and to the rest of the world.

INTRODUCTION

I have chosen to write about the area within the Ring of Fire, a vast region of the Pacific that is often the source of earthquakes, volcanoes, tsunamis, and other disruptions on our planet Mother Earth. When her stomachaches, she reacts. We can stimulate this by feeding her thoughtless acts of violence and pollution.

In ancient times Mother Earth was a perfect Being of beauty and a place of peace and harmony. It would seem reasonable that if Mother Earth, who is no longer perfect, can be turned toward perfection, then there is less risk of disruptions in the Ring of Fire.

How can we do this?

By raising the consciousness of humanity so its actions will be peaceful and loving.

This is easier said than done. However, we have tools to help us. All have a consciousness. All are One. All actions affect All. Give love to the flowers in your garden and your flowers will love you. Give love to the animals and the birds and the trees and they will respond with love. Mother Earth has a consciousness, and so, when we humans behave in a loving manner, she feels this. When we behave in an unloving manner, she feels this, too.

The great healer is Love. Mother Earth heals when she feels Love expressed by humanity.

In ancient times Lemurians lived on Mother Earth and they held strongly the concept of Love for all. These vibrations, frequencies, energies remain.

Memory holds all deeds. Memory is part of mass consciousness that unites all of us. What you think, what I think, is part of a great soup pot of mass consciousness drunk by all. All affects All because All are One.

My thought is to introduce you to Lemurian energies so you may feel these Love energies that remain in the memory. Once you have felt them, once you know them, then you can spread them across the land to help heal Mother Earth.

"Kirael: Lemurian Legacy for the Great Shift", written by Fred Sterling, gives much information on the Lemurians. Primarily, they lived in the region of the Pacific, and although today most of the land is submerged, there remain the tops of mountains in the form of islands.

What are the vibrations of these places?

Assuming that the actions of the Lemurians have put down loving vibrations, then that is what will be found on the land. Remember, all is held within the memory. If some vibrations are found to be imperfect, then there is need for restoration.

This is not as difficult as you may think. With the mind, one can create a reality of perfection to lay on the vibrations of the land of today. Remember, energy IS. It exists. Because it exists, it must be counted. Therefore, to overlay a new perfection of reality is an act that must be counted. It is recorded in the memories of the All. Since the energies of peace and health and especially the energies of Love were uppermost in the minds of the Lemurians, it is logical that these energies are used for restoration.

Over the years, I have kept a journal of my travels, and now I am opening to my travels in the Pacific area. We need to look at the Ring of Fire. We need to feel the Lemurian energies of Love that heal, and we need to begin restoring what we find is not perfect.

My goal is to use techniques that will ultimately help the entire planet become more peaceful, more healthy, more loving. Techniques used in one place can be used in other places. The Ring of Fire is a good place to begin. However, for one moment, let us put the project on hold. I have met the legacy of the Lemurians themselves. It was only a brief encounter, at Mount Shasta, California, on the edge of the Ring of Fire. With that in mind, join me as I relate this meeting and then I will take you to the islands of Hawaii, center of the Ring of Fire, to a specific island, Kauai, where the Love vibrations from the ancient times of Lemuria are still strongly imprinted on the land.

CHAPTER 1

Mount Shasta, Meeting the Lemurians

September 23, The Equinox:

It is fire season when I am driving a rental car down a California mountain road, my husband reclining in the back seat recovering from hernia surgery and our friend Hal in the front passenger seat pointing the way. We are headed toward Mount Shasta on a beautiful, clear morning, and even the smoke earlier shrouding the mountains to the southeast has retreated. We are able to see on these neighboring mountains outlines of tall green pines and a gash of autumn bright yellow-orange here and there. Beautiful scenery.

Today is the Autumn Equinox and our destination is Mount Shasta because it is a living model of mystery where the past, present, and future fuse. I am excited to visit this place. It is my first time here, but I know this is a magical place. To actually be at the mountain itself brings a quickening to my heart, an excitement hard to describe.

Just now, however, I am paying special attention to the road, with a bit of anxiety mixed with my excitement because there are no guard rails lining this mountain road and I am thinking that a sudden mistake would send us plunging. I ask our California friend how he can drive this road in the winter, and he is saying that the rain changes to snow only near the top, and he does not live here in the winter.

I feel relief when we are off the mountain road, driving on smooth, paved Scott River Road with a gentle, twisting river beside us. Where I live, we would call it a stream. A couple days ago, it was hidden by smoke. I am thinking of the fish in this river/stream, and suddenly I see a blue heron. Fishing, probably. Beautiful scenery! How different is our experience today from a couple days ago when my husband and I were following with great anxiety a pickup truck as it made its way through dense smoke to reach the mountain road that would take us to the top, to the home of our California friend.

With the smoke gone today, we see For Sale signs in front of small ranch houses. Our friend says the economy is depressed here. This is cattle country and we see barns and fences, and yes, some cattle are grazing, even some sheep, and, yes, look to the left, a rancher has just begun to cut his crop of grain. We are going along slowly, looking at this beautiful countryside, and finally we come to a ranger station and a modern supermarket called Gils Market. We are at the town of Fort Jones. A big sign, 'Thank you, Fire Fighters!' is draped above the main street. I slow the car a bit when our friend warns me to be mindful of the local sheriff who takes a dim view of speeding.

Soon the road begins to climb and when the climb becomes steep, I shift to a lower gear. The little rental car does not have much power. We reach the town of Yreka, pass McDonalds, turn onto I-5 Expressway, and head south toward Mount Shasta. Now we are expectantly looking for the big mountain, but we do not see it. On clear days, says our friend, he can see it from his neighbor's house.

The sky is becoming overcast, and as we drive closer to Mount Shasta, the sky is becoming more and more overcast and we are beginning to see cars coming toward us with headlights shining. Oh dear! To our left, is that Shasta? I am looking at a shrouded, tall, twin-peaked mountain close to the road. No, says our friend, not Shasta. He is expressing amazement that we cannot see Shasta.

Finally a road sign tells us to leave this good road if we want to go to the town of Mount Shasta, and we obey this road sign and quickly we are arriving at the town. Its Western-style wide streets are clean and orderly. The main intersection is at Lake and Mount Shasta Boulevards, and a big Shell station stands at the corner. I park our rental car and we begin looking for a bookstore with spiritual tendencies. Our friend has told us there is such a bookstore. Yes, here it is, and we enter this place and we are greeted by strong, spiritual energy reminding me of the Edgar Cayce center in Virginia Beach.

A man and woman run this bookstore, both strongly occult, as one would expect, both strongly intuitive. The man is young, late twenties, tall and thin. I ask him the direction for Mount Shasta and he is explaining how one can get up the mountain by taking this road and that road and turning here and there. When he finishes, I face the front window and ask if this is the direction for Mount Shasta. Yes.

The pull of the mountain is so strong, I find it unusual not to be able to see it. Before entering the bookstore, we three have joked that we are probably the first to come to Mount Shasta and not see it. Well, of course our friend has seen it many times.

I am now leaving the bookstore, walking alone up Lake Street toward the mountain I cannot see, looking for a good place to meditate, walking along the Western street, so clean and orderly, walking slowly up a gradual incline, knowing I am at the foot of the big mountain, looking at the flowers and the green grass in front of the small, neat houses, looking for a good place to meditate, and yes, just ahead, just beyond the last house, just over there under a roadside tree, yes, that will be a good place. The tree overhanging the road will give shade to the car.

I return to the bookstore and arrange to meet my husband and friend later, and then I am taking the rental car and driving up Lake to the place where the tree overhangs the street at the foot of the big mountain I cannot see, and I am parking the car with the front passenger window open to give air. There is need for an open window. It is hot.

11:15 a.m., on this day of the Autumn Equinox, I begin meditating, facing the big mountain with its big vibrations, thinking on this mountain. No, that is not exactly correct. I am thinking on the Lemurians. I have been thinking on the Lemurians since I entered the bookstore, when the first meeting with the man made a link between the present human race and the Lemurians. His vibrations have told me that. I have seen that.

The Lemurians are in the mountain in front of me. I cannot see them with my physical eyes, but I know they are there. I begin meditating, removing myself from the third dimension, entering the vibrations of this place. So strong are the vibrations of the Lemurians! And yes, this strength raises my energies high, high, high! Such strength, this place!

Such LIGHT! I can see this with my inner eye. And yes, I am entering the council chamber of the Lemurians. They are accepting me, but not as one of them. I know this. I am an accepted visitor. We are celebrating the Autumn Equinox together. No, wrong word. We are not celebrating. We are working. We are working for Mother Earth!

It is coming close to twelve noon now and I am turning my thoughts away from the Lemurians, focusing on Libra, yes, Libra, the Lords of Libra, they who bring strong Light, strong balance at the Equinox. And I am also thinking on the Pleiadians, our brothers. And I am also thinking on the Lords of Sirius, yes, yes, they who help our planet. And yes, I am thinking on the Light of Buddha and on the Light of the Christ and on the others. I am combining the power of all who help us.

All that Light is coming down at noon of the Autumn Equinox to Mount Shasta where the Lemurians are uniting to make this place strong, strong with the vibrant thought form of LOVE.

Now this united, powerful Light of LOVE is spread throughout all of Mother Earth.

I return to the bookstore, and when I open the door, the man who operates the bookstore and I look at each other. He is the link between the present human race and the Lemurians. We do not speak. There is no need to speak because we understand. It is time to leave the bookstore with my husband and friend.

In the night, when I am in the Astral with the Lemurians, I am with a man, tall, thin, similar in many ways to the man in the bookstore. He gives me a book, small, square, thick with large print and a sturdy cover with tiny stones attached to it. There are nine small stones. With the man is a woman of French-Canadian features, dark hair, pale complexion as if she has never seen the sun, wearing an Angora sweater embedded with many tiny pearls. Her sweater reminds me of the fashion style of years ago. She begins telling me about the past of the Lemurians and I am interrupting her. I do not want to talk about the past. That is not important just now. What is important is <u>today</u>. Today is the time of the great crisis.

Curious, these people of yesterday who have a different concept of time from we present humans. They think in terms of immense blocks of time. Strange to have worked with them in the council chamber.

It is now the next day, Thursday, the 24th, and I am in my noon meditation. I am thinking for a moment of the Lemurians in their council chamber, and I am surprised they are not in the chamber. When I question their absence, the Higher Worlds tell me it is not the Equinox and so they are not in their council chamber at this hour. I am surprised because I have assumed they will always be in their council chamber.

CHAPTER 2

Kauai, Island of Love

Now I am ready to visit the island of Love, as I call Kauai, a Hawaiian island I think retains perfection inherited from ancient Lemuria. I expect to find Love in the land, in the mountains, the trees, the flowers, and yes, in humans who dwell here. This is my first visit and I am impatient to learn whether or not I am correct.

If I meet the legacy of Love, then I will use it to overlay faulty reality needing to be changed. That is what one can do. It is not necessary to call in a crowd to help. Yes, mass consciousness on a mass basis would be helpful, but one has to be practical. If one is alone, then one must begin with the Self, and with the knowledge that All is One, All is Mass Consciousness. I can create a reality of perfection and overlay it on reality needing to be changed with the realization that the thought form produced REMAINS. It is energy. Crack open the door to a new possibility and have the FAITH that the energy of creating a reality will attract itself to those whose job it is to help change the situation. That is how it is done.

In any case, just before evening, 5 p.m., I have arrived at Lihue Airport on the island of Kauai, and I am waiting to speak with the manager of American International Car Rentals who is on the phone refusing a rental car to someone. When she hangs up, she tells me there are only two rental cars left, and do I want one of them? I hesitate. I do not need a car tonight, but I will need one tomorrow. She says planes will arrive on the island for another two hours and who knows whether the two remaining cars will be rented and whether there will be a rental car available for me tomorrow morning. I am tired. I do not want to bother with a rental car today. I decide to take my chances tomorrow.

A taxi driver takes me two miles to where I have made reservations with Spike, a carpenter by trade, who has built his own hotel. The driver, as we are going along, glances at me in the mirror and asks why I am staying at Spike's place when a woman like me should be staying in town so I can walk up and down the streets and see things. I shrug my shoulders.

He takes me along a good asphalt road with no traffic and stops in front of a small, triple-decker complex with no identifying sign. We have arrived. I am looking at this place out here alone without a sign, pickup trucks parked in front, wondering if I have made a mistake. I pay the taxi driver and he gives me a ripe yellow papaya, cautioning me to take out the seeds before eating it. Seeds aren't eaten, he warns. I am thanking him, knowing that tonight my supper will be his papaya and my dry food from home.

An Hawaiian man looking fifty with a square face is standing in the yard next to a large, white fishing boat hoisted onto a rack. I ask if he is Spike. Yes, and as he smiles, his eyes become slits. All his face becomes slits. Lots of slits on that face. Good face. Kind man.

We enter his hotel that has no sign and we go to his small concrete block office that is functional, not fancy. A waterway for carp comes into the office from an outside pool and I am greeting the fish. Big yellow, orange, black, multi-colored carp. Spike says they can live 200 years. He tells me he has to clean his carp pool often because the algae grows very fast in the pool, and then he adds in a joking way that maybe the carp like the algae in order to hide from the people. But the fish aren't hiding from me. I am talking to them and they are coming to see what all this is about.

Spike gives me the key to Room 9 on the second floor, and I am finding my room by climbing an outside concrete stairway between buildings. As I climb, what do I see here? A concrete covered water causeway attached to many narrow water pipes. Why? My room has lost its number tag, but '9' is penciled on the door, so I know my key will fit the lock. I enter the room, which is quite large and has a small refrigerator. Good. Also, there is a balcony. Spike's place has interested me because of the balcony. I am looking out at a parking area of pickup trucks and old cars and beyond these is the street with no traffic, then a pink flowering hedge and bushes, and then untamed sandy ground with low bushes and palm trees. Beyond this is the ocean. Yes, the blue blue ocean. That is what I want to see. Yes, this place, Spike's place, is exactly where I want to be.

I sleep well and wake as dawn begins. A somewhat red sky is in the East with the sun thinking about rising from the dark ocean. The remainder of the sky is black. I am lying with my head at the foot of the bed looking out, the balcony glass door open, screen in place to keep out mosquitoes, and I am hearing them buzzing to get into this warm room. It is cold outside and they are sensing the warmth, and probably me.

It is quiet, very quiet. The birds are not yet awake. I am looking at the stars in the black sky. So many of them. Bright, bright. I wait for the black ocean to begin turning to dark blue, and now I am beginning to see the outlines of palm trees sharp against the dark sea. I am watching all this, and yes, I am thinking this is exactly where I should be, at Spike's place. Not in the town. A man comes out of the darkness, goes to a pickup truck, starts it, and drives away. Soon another and then another. Time for work here on this island of Kauai. I am lying here on my bed, watching.

7:15 a.m., I am with Spike in his office and he is phoning American International Car Rentals. The man who answers says there is a car for me. Only one to choose from. No air conditioning. Am I satisfied? Yes. Someone from the rental office will come for me, and within ten minutes a young man is at Spike's place to pick me up. He drives me through the quiet countryside, avoiding the town of Lihue, and at the airport, a little red Nissan is waiting for me. The man at the rental office is shaking his head in disbelief as he hands me the keys. He says just before Spike called asking about a rental car for me, the manager has phoned him to say that a Barbara Wolf at the Ocean View Motel will phone and she is to have the only remaining rental car. And yes, Spike has phoned less than two minutes later. Thank you, Higher Worlds! I have my rental car! The rental man is still shaking his head in disbelief as I drive away.

This little red car will see much driving. I intend to intensely feel the vibrations of this island of Kauai that I call the island of Love in order to experience the vibrations of ancient Lemuria. My first priority will be to drive in the mountains to see Mt.Waialeale. Its name means overflowing water, an appropriate name for a mountain receiving the most rain in all the world. A clean mountain, I am thinking. After a shower, one feels clean. This will be a clean mountain. Clean vibrations.

Today, as I begin my journey to this mountain, the land is bathed in sunshine. Perfect.

I am driving along, and as I climb upwards, my little car gives me magnificent views of mountains and canyons. I am trying to identify which mountain is Waialeale. I cannot be certain, but the scenery is gorgeous! Breathtaking! The vibrations are very good. When I reach a great height, I stop at a lookout to see the deep blue ocean far below. But I must be mindful of the weather. I have been warned about fog. It can come in fast, and when I first glimpse it, I must begin to drive down. Yes, I see it and so I begin going down fast. Cold air comes with it. Yes, it is definitely time to leave the mountains.

When I reach the coastal road, I stop at a small town, Waimea, to look at a statue of Captain Cook. I park the little red Nissan and walk across a small patch of grass to the statue to read a sign explaining that the first foreign landing on Hawaiian soil was January 20, 1778.

January 20! This is a shock! January 20 is the first day of Aquarius, signaling the first day of a New Age, Aquarius is the constellation that joins the two halves -- East and West. How interesting that Captain Cook landed on January 20! Now interesting I am here reading this sign.

I pause for a moment to drink in the significance of this before I ask a passerby for directions to the Menehune Ditch. He indicates a tiny sign just beyond the Captain Cook statue pointing the way to Menehune Ditch. Oh! I had not seen this tiny sign.

I am following instructions and I am driving now on a rough road, passing small houses showing little prosperity, passing a small Buddhist temple, coming to a newly constructed suspension footbridge for crossing a river. The bridge is made of treated lumber, suspended by ropes, and I know it will swing back and forth when used. I am thinking of the Burma bridges I have seen in the movies, this one being much smaller than the ones in the movies. Yes, after I find the Menehune Ditch, I will walk on the swinging bridge. I have never done this. Here is my chance to experience.

But where is the Menehune Ditch? The guidebook says it is at the bridge. I have parked my car and I look for a wall rather than a ditch because the guidebook says the ditch is constructed with rocks closely set together without mortar, as is found at the ancient South American site of Tiahuanaco. I look at the cliffs on my side of the river, craning my neck, looking here and there, not seeing a wall.

An old truck slowly approaches and I put up my hand for it to stop. It does. This truck is towing a wooden flat bed holding two horses, and the back of the truck itself holds a pack of hunting dogs half asleep, their heads resting on the wooden truck sides They are sleepily looking at me as if to ask, what does this dumb woman want?

I ask the truck man where is the Menehune Ditch and I am looking up at the cliffs, ready for his answer. He tells me I am standing on it. Oh! I look down and see two tiers of rocks at the edge of the road, all that remains of the ancient work. The old truck with the bored dogs and two horses starts up and leaves and I begin examining what remains of the Menehune Ditch walls. I note that yes indeed, the construction is the same as at Tiahuanaco, the rocks fitting to each other so tightly that no water can seep through this waterway. How was this done? How were the rules bent to make the waterway? Who created something so unique that stones without mortar can prevent water leakage? True, this Menehune Ditch work is cruder than what I have seen in South America. Yet, the result is the same -- perfectly fitted stones.

A man and woman are parking their car and coming to see the wall. We begin speaking, speculating on who has built it, and then the woman points out a natural large hole in the cliff beside the wall. We speculate that this large hole would be where water would pass though to supply the original waterway, or ditch. We wonder whether this waterway was originally built to irrigate crops.

When the couple leaves, I turn my attention to the suspension bridge, and I am climbing the construction and walking halfway across the bridge, it swinging slightly from my weight. I am looking down at the trees on the opposite bank, trees hanging over the water, and I am looking at big green fruit hanging from one tree. So much to eat here on this tropical island, if one knows what is edible. A short way beyond the bridge I am watching a truck fording the river, its motor grinding. It is crossing the river where stones have been placed to build up the bed. I am watching the truck cross the river but my mind is on the Menehune Ditch.

I return to the wall to pickup a stone and place it in my hand. Then I put my hand flat on the wall to take in the vibrations of the wall built in former times. I want these vibrations. Now I am speaking in telepathy to those around me. They have been with me most of the day, and now they are here in <u>droves</u>. Little people. I have been all day excusing myself for inadvertently stepping on them. They are not being hurt by me because they are in the fourth dimension, the Astral, and my body is in the third dimension. Nevertheless, when I step on them, I say I am sorry. They are tiny, not coming above my knees. Short and stout. That is my description of them. And they are similarly dressed, like the dwarfs of the Snow White myth, wearing pointed hats. Now I am asking them in telepathy whether they, the Menehune, have built this ditch. I am not given a straight answer. Well, never mind. These little people, dwarfs, gnomes, friendly little things, no higher than to my knees, are <u>all</u> <u>over</u> <u>the</u> <u>place</u>!

What are we dealing with here? Legend has it that Kauai is the home of the little people called Menehune. They live in the mountains and can perform great engineering feats from stone. Legend has it that when the first wave of settlers settled in Hawaii, these settlers had the Menehune build irrigation causeways and fish ponds.

Are these little people former Lemurians? I do not think they are former Lemurians. Maybe their thought form was constructed by the Lemurians. I do not know, but one thing I do know, they are friendly, very friendly. If they like to work, then they should be invited to help with the restoration of Mother Earth.

A note here:

Several years after I meet the Menehunes, I am in Switzerland with two friends and we are driving in the Alps when we come to a sign warning that the road ahead is blocked because of an avalanche. Never mind. The Swiss are good at solving such problems. They have dug a tunnel through the mountain to build a train track. We approach the tunnel just as a train of flatbed cars is ready to depart, and we drive onto the last flatbed and wait patiently in our car as the train takes us through the tunnel. We were riding along when I feel a Presence behind me and I turn to see a trail of dwarfs flying in a straight line following our flatbed. Amazing! The little friendly ones are not confined to Hawaii!

As for the Menehune Ditch, here on this island of Kauai, probably it was built by the Menehunes, but this construction was not for them. It was for those who lived and commanded here. I put in my pocket the stone I have picked up and I drive away from the Menehune Ditch in my little red Nissan rental car.

Now I am headed to a place called Salt Pond that has a little park with green grass and a sandy beach just beyond for bathers. My thought is to visit the beach, and when I arrive at Salt Pond, I park the car and begin walking on the grass. It feels good to walk on the grass. An old Hawaiian man approaches me with a smile, says hello and introduces himself as Uncle Louie. He wants to know if this is my first time in Hawaii. I am a bit startled by his question as I answer that it is indeed my first time. This tall, old man calling himself Uncle Louie has a Hawaiian face full of smiles and a pair of blue eyes, and now he is asking my name. When I tell him it is Barbara, this is not good enough for him. I must have a Hawaiian name. I watch him considering for a moment before he names me 'Palla Palla'. That will be my name. I like the name.

Now Uncle Louie is asking where I am staying and I say at Spike's place. He is pleased, and he tells me Spike is a good man, a very good man. I agree and Uncle Louie asks me to say hello to Spike for him.

It is my turn to ask Uncle Louie about himself, and he says he used to drive a tourist bus but now he is in charge of this place. He turns on the sprinklers. I am looking at the sprinklers and the small birds taking baths at the sprinklers. He cleans up the place, and yes, I can see that. He talks with the people, and yes, that is evident. What fun it is to talk with this man of Love!

Suddenly Uncle Louie points to the parking area and tells me to wave good-bye to his friend Edie. I look at an old man at the wheel of a decrepit yellow car leaving the area and I am waving to him. Uncle Louie is waving also, and the man is seeing us and waving. Then I am feeling Uncle Louie's arm come around my back, his hand lightly touching my shoulder, he standing very close to me. I am willing to play the game of fun, and I am leaning against his chest, putting my head lightly on his shoulder, waving gaily to his friend Edie in the old yellow car. Edie, his eyes as big as saucers, is seeing his friend Uncle Louie with this strange woman, and his old yellow car is nearly running into parked cars as he is laughing and waving and laughing and waving. Then he gives us the Hawaiian good-bye sign of the little finger and thumb. At least I hope it is the Hawaiian good-bye sign. I copy him, and we are all laughing and having fun, laughing and having fun.

A moment of Love.

That is what the Lemurians knew. They have left us a good legacy here.

I leave Uncle Louie to go to the sandy beach to watch the people sunbathing, some swimming. Such a happy place. Uncle Louie sees to that. Then I return to walk on the grass, passing the sprinklers with the happy bathing birds, and I am saying good-bye to Uncle Louie, and climbing into my little red Nissan to drive away from this happy place. Yes, this is a beautiful legacy of the Lemurians.

It is time to find Puhi Road, and I am recognizing the turnoff as the one I used earlier this morning. Puhi Road is a narrow road going through sugar cane fields, the canes so tall they crowd the road and dwarf my rental car. I remember earlier today seeing great machines reaping the sugar cane, syrupy red liquid running down the crushing machines, a sickly smell of crushed cane penetrating my nostrils. Huge trucks filled with cane wait their turn. Yes, I have

It is hot on this narrow road with the towering cane leaning over the road threatening in my imagination to crush my little red car. I am going along until I spot far below me a big pond, the Menehune Fish Pond, and I am stopping to look at it. Below the pond is a river. I am looking at a place where the river has been diked by the strange stone wall formation of long ago. The bushes hide the wall but I know I am looking at the big Menehune Fish Pond. I see fish swirls.

I am looking at the entire scenery of fish pond, river and high mountains with their sharp green outlines. Friendly mountains, not heavy with trees or brush, yet, green mountains going down to the sea. There is something very nice about these mountains. I am remembering they are the same mountains I have seen from Spike's place. They are the homes of the little people who thrive on Love, as did the Lemurians, as does Uncle Louie and his friend Edie.

I am driving down the road toward the sea, toward the harbor, toward Spike's place, and when I reach the level of the sea, I am passing a small harbor, very small harbor, and here is a steel gray small warship docked at the port. American. At the fenced gate of this tiny harbor are armed American sailors. Strange to see American sailors with guns. I have never seen American sailors with guns guarding anywhere. Here they are, thousands of miles from home. Hawaii does not feel like a state. No, not at all. Except for the roads. Yes, it is strange to see armed, white-uniformed American sailors guarding their steel gray warship. I am passing the harbor and the armed American sailors and their steel gray warship and very quickly I am at Spike's place.

Big meditation today. I am bringing down the Light for <u>all</u> of the Pacific, with this island called Kauai at the center. The meditation brings a big response, even more than yesterday when I concentrated mostly on helping the island to respond, and yes, it did respond yesterday! Today I am concentrating on the Pacific. The Light is coming down to the island, and I am spreading it out to all of the Pacific.

Interesting how easy it is to make this place called Kauai respond, and I am knowing that much as been done here previously. How long ago does not matter. Once done, always it will respond again. It only needs to be tapped. <u>There was much done here before</u>!!!! I am thinking on those who did the work before. Yet, that is not entirely correct. I am not trying to penetrate the veil that separates this knowledge from me. No, let it be. Now it is my time. Let the past rest. Use it, yes. Use the tools, but do not look at the details. Use the tool of Love. Use a mixture of Love and humor.

I am up early, before dawn, looking out my screened porch (lanai is the word the Hawaiians use) at the stars in the dark sky. Orion high overhead and Sirius and Aldebaran and the others, and I am knowing that the Pleiades cluster is out there but I cannot locate it.

Now to sleep again for a short time before wakening to a high pitched noise! What is that noise? Oh dear! I am trying to locate the noise and yes, it is coming from the industrial plant across the street from the harbor. Sugar cane plant. I realize now that it was closed for the weekend, but now, 8 a.m., Monday morning, it is screeching!

After breakfast, I drive the little red Nissan along the harbor road and when I reach the harbor I see the naval ship is gone. After the harbor, I pass a sign advertising deep sea fishing, and I am going along slowly to Puhi Road to see again the Menehune Fish Pond.

I stop a moment to look at the pond far below me. Fish are jumping. One duck is on the pond. Further down on the bank of the river is a small house with smoke coming up. I think someone is cooking fish for breakfast. A tourist bus stops near my little red Nissan and tourists crane their necks to see the fish pond. After a moment, the tourist bus goes away and I am alone, looking at the fish pond in the quiet of the morning, not yet hot, smoke coming lazily straight up from the house on the river bank. Beyond the river are the green, green mountains going down to the sea. Something special about those mountains, their features so sharply etched against the sky. Something special.

Yesterday there were so many little people! Where have they gone? I do not see any. Yesterday I stumbled over them and now they are gone. They are in the mountains.

I am leaving this perfect spot, this view of the fish pond with the smoke coming straight up from the house and the etched green mountains, and I am driving through the cane fields, the road very, very narrow. Big red sugar cane trucks are again active this morning. I am stopping at a fruit stand to buy a ripe papaya from a man looking like an ex-seaman who says he has been on the island for years and years and years. This man warns me that the papaya I have just bought should be eaten today. Bright yellow fruit. Soft. Yes, I understand what he is saying. This papaya is ripe. Tomorrow it will be spoiled. Yes, the papaya will be eaten for lunch.

I am looking now for Route 50, hoping to take that road to reach Makahuena Point where Spike says there are petroglyphs that probably will be covered with sand. When I reach a rough gravel road, I stop. My interest is not so strong that I will drive a rental car on this rough road. I turn around and go a short way to Poipu Beach Park, a green, well-kept park, and soon I am walking across the green to a golden sand beach. A perfect place to swim! A black lava reef forms a natural, shallow bathing pool for children. Beautiful, clear water here! I touch the water and it is warm. I <u>must</u> swim here.

My swimsuit is in the car and I soon have it on and am swimming in this wonderful natural pool. Never mind that it is shallow. It does not have to be deep. I laze a long time in this shallow place, scooping up golden sand and patting it on my body. Warm, gentle, beautiful, blue Pacific. It is the first time for me to swim in this ocean. I am sitting on the bottom lazily patting golden sand on my skin. Paradise!

Now I am putting on my clothes and driving the red Nissan a short distance, just up the road, to the Kiahun Plantation Gardens, an extensive, tropical garden, so lush, so well cared for, gardeners here and there, and I am walking on these grounds, stopping at small ponds to see orange and black carp, reading signs saying not to feed the carp because they have a special diet. There are also black fish here. What are they? And tiny pools of lily pads with red flowers.

And flowering shrubs rimming the grassy areas. Hanging fruit. So fragrant are the aromas of the flowers and the fruit! Oh, Hawaii, you are <u>so</u> nice!

And yes, I must look at the large cactus garden here in this garden complex. Huge cactus of many types. But, oh, the fragrance of the rain forest flowers! These I like the best. I am leaving this beautiful garden complex, returning to Spike's place, passing the Menehune Fish Pond one more time, looking at the green mountains beyond the river, and when I arrive at Spike's place, the high pitched noise of the sugar cane plant is gone. The factory is idle. Good!

In Room 9 at Spike's place, 12 noon, a <u>big</u> meditation, <u>big</u> Light coming down, big acupuncture needle between the heavens and the earth. Kauai, today, right smack in the center!

Easy, easy to do this because others have done it before. Yes, this land has been well worked.

Lunch is my papaya. Very good.

This afternoon, gentle rain, not cold. Persistent rain. In between the rain, Spike is painting white his boat called Christmas, and he is telling me about his boat as he is painting. After he bought it, a tourist has asked when it would be ready for launching, and he gave the date of Christmas. Later, the tourist wrote him asking about Christmas, and at first Spike did not understand. As he tells me this story, his face is all smiles and slits. Christmas? Who is Christmas, he is relating to me. Then he realizes the tourist is referring to his boat, and so Spike has named his boat Christmas.

I am telling Spike about Uncle Louie and Edie and how Uncle Louie has said to give his regards to Spike, and Spike is telling me with great humor how Uncle Louie had tried to put one over on him. He says some tourists staying at his place had met Uncle Louie in a similar manner as I had met him, and these tourists were telling Uncle Louie about staying at Spike's place and how wonderful was Spike's large Kauai shell collection. Uncle Louie told the tourists he had one Kauai shell that Spike did not have, and he gave this shell to the tourists to give to Spike. Innocently they presented it to Spike and Spike looked at it and told them the shell is not from Kauai, but from Quadulane. Even today this amusing incident produces a big horse laugh from both Spike and Uncle Louie when they review their storage boxes of memories.

Storage boxes of humorous memories are what ripens the fruit of this island. The fruit of Love. Love and humor. Love, humor, and health. What fun it is for me to experience these spoken memories!

As Spike is painting Christmas, he tells me about the man whose indoor cactus is almost the size of his house and he does not know what to do. He decides to charge 25 cents for people to see the cactus, and the people come and pay. Soon many people come, and so he starts charging 50 cents. Still they come. Spike says even his sister pays to see the cactus and by that time the price is up to one dollar. Spike is laughing, his face full of smiles and slits, saying, now so many are coming, the man is making $18,000 a year!

Spike tells me about the wealthy man living on the island who tears the ads out of his almanac so he could read his almanac without being disturbed by ads. He tells me about another man who has no secretary and whose papers and letters are scattered over his office floor so Spike has to jump over them when he visits. The man claims he knows where every paper is.

Spike's face, as he tells me these stories, shows he is a happy man, a happy human living on this island that was once the homeland of the Lemurians who believed in Love. Love and humor.

Now Spike is showing me a pool of carp beside the hotel. These are big fish, and I am understanding that somehow these big fish can swim through the concrete tanks at the back of the hotel. One of the tank coverings is off and I can see the carp. It is so strange seeing this arrangement of concrete tanks and many small water pipes at the back of the hotel! Only Spike could have built such a thing. With the help of the little people, maybe.

———◆———

I wake early and the black sky has many bright stars but I do not recognize them. I wait for sunup so I can see the bushes with big pink flowers across the street, and the big green mountains sharply etched against the sky. I have breakfast in my room as I look out at the island. This morning will be my last look at the island before I fly to Maui.

I am ready to leave too early, and so I talk with Spike who is standing next to Christmas.

He tells me about the three men who drifted at sea with a broken motor for three days and the Coast Guard could not find them. Nor could the search planes. Finally the boats and planes gave up, except a plane flown by the brother-in-law of one of the lost men. This flier continued searching, making a careful circle, always going a bit farther north because of the direction of the drift created by the trade winds, and this brother-in-law found them. Spike told me they cried on the boat, as if this was a terrible thing. He repeated this several times, and I told him that the men thought they would die.

Spike has another story ready for me. Later he was at sea with one of these same men and the boat motor broke. Spike was seasick from the motion of the drifting boat and he had gone to sleep. While he was asleep, his friend fixed the motor and they were going in the dark toward shore when the motor broke again. Spike woke and quickly threw the anchor overboard and the boat held firm. Then he was sick again from the motion of the stricken boat and he went to sleep. His friend again fixed the motor and when it was fixed, his friend pulled up the anchor. Spike had awakened as they were coming to shore. He told me he was amazed that the man had pulled up the anchor without Spike realizing this.

Spike's parents were waiting in the dark at the shore for him and they had been very stern with him. I said they were afraid, and I have asked, why didn't he have a radio? There was a radio, Spike told me it was broken and he had not realized this. He shook his head, still in amazement that this incident should have happened to his friend who had almost died at sea just a short time before. Spike told me he himself has never again gone to sea without first checking the radio and this and that. Interesting, this man Spike. Much character in his face from a hard life. Seven years working in Alaska, he told me. A long time to be away from Hawaii.

I say good-bye to him in the parking lot and I drive my red Nissan to the airport, turn it in, check in at the airline counter, and what is this? A plane is leaving right now for Maui via Honolulu? Do I want to go on this plane or wait for mine? Well, why not go on this plane via Honolulu. I check my suitcase and board the plane.

Readers, I have reserved Chapter 5 for my experiences on Oahu.

CHAPTER 3

Maui, Island of the Sun

We are flying toward Maui over the blue, blue of the Pacific, so calm, so peaceful, and quickly we are seeing land below us. I am looking down at the island of Molokai as we fly the length of this island, home of dark priests in the old days. I feel a certain inhospitality in the vibrations of this place, inhospitality left over from the old days of the dark priests. Very little Light here.

The land looks dry. I see a plot of cultivated land here and there, but on the whole, the place does not seem developed. Later, I am told that Hawaiians afflicted by leprosy were gathered up and sent to Molokai to live out their lives. Even today descendants of these unfortunate people are still living in Molokai. I am looking down at this island and thinking it is strange that there should be this island with dubious vibrations amid the good vibrations of the other islands.

Now the pilot is pointing out the island of Lanai and I am looking down at it. In a short time we are flying over the island of Maui and landing at the Kahului airport, my destination.

The airport is small, airy. I am walking to the tourist desk, taking a visitor's brochure, then picking up my suitcase and walking across the street to the Budget rental car booth to board a van to the rental lot. Businessmen ride with me. At the rental lot, I am given a two-door, blue Nissan, and yes, this is very acceptable. I am driving it away, heading toward the town of Kahului, following directions on a map beside me on the passenger's seat. Yes, here is what I am looking for, the Maui Huluki Hotel, Hawaiian owned. I am given a room on the second floor, Number

204, overlooking a fresh water swimming pool planted in the middle of a green lawn bordered by palm trees at one end and the beach and blue Pacific at the other end. Far beyond the pool, towering high, high, are spectacular green mountains. A beautiful setting!

The beach looks somewhat muddy. No golden sands of Kauai here. A small, white plastic jug is floating offshore. The hotel pool beckons me more than the beach, and I take a long, lazy swim in this wonderful pool. When I climb out, a wagon of fresh white towels is waiting for me.

At noon in my room I meditate, and I am examining the Maui vibrations that are new to me. They feel subtly different from Kauai vibrations. Yes, the vibrations of this new place I am visiting are nice, but, on first impression, these vibrations lack the mystery, the unknown of the Kauai vibrations. That is a strange way to explain the Maui vibrations. What am I missing? What is different? Lemurian vibrations of Love so strongly within the vibrations of Kauai are missing here at Maui. That is what I am missing.

After meditation, lunch of my food from home and a rest before I take a short drive to the Maui Zoological and Botanical Gardens. I stop first at the zoo and note that the cages are too small for the monkeys and peacocks. There is enough room for the black swans, but, as for the others, the accommodations are too small and not well serviced. Fortunately, few animals are confined to this place of dubious happiness.

Now I walk along pathways in the nearby Botanical Garden. Most of the plants are not in bloom and I think probably it is the wrong time of year for that. Very dry, the garden and zoo. How different from Kauai.

I am leaving this place, heading towards the Valley of Iao on a road called by that name, and I am following it upwards. The land is lush and green. I am stopping briefly at Kepaniwai Park, a pretty green little place, to walk to the Chinese pagoda being guarded by two large white ceramic mythical lions. So Chinese is the feeling of this place! A good feeling. I am walking to the fish pond and Japanese pavilion commemorating those who came to Hawaii years ago to work at the sugar cane plantations and remained here.

Now I continue driving toward Iao Needle, this place of great interest to me because it is an acupuncture needle that can be used to stimulate energies for the benefit of peace and health for Mother Earth. Significantly, this acupuncture needle is in Hawaii, center of the ancient lands of Lemuria. I am driving along a narrow roadway looking at magnificent, high green mountains and I see Iao Needle, the big green acupuncture needle, towering above me. I park my little blue Nissan to begin walking on the pathways of this lush place, looking up at this big green acupuncture needle called Iao Needle, and then I pick up a volcanic stone. This stone will be excellent for magnetizing this place during meditation.

I am climbing here and there amid lush tropical green foliage, up steps, down steps, many steps, and, yes, I am spending a long time here in this beautiful, towering, green place.

Male vibrations are here. Warriors. Some with the killing blood. Well, sorry, guys, I am not paying attention to you today. I am here for Mother Earth, at her acupuncture needle, to be used as a tool for stimulating her.

———————◆———————

Full Moon Day:

Today I will visit Haleakala Crater, called House of the Sun, and I am thinking of our sun whose energies sustain life on our planet. The name House of the Sun points to an intimate relationship between our sun and this place, Haleakala, located at the center of ancient Lemuria, a place of Love. To understand the vibrations of Haleakala opens a door, puts a tool in my hands for helping our planet.

7:45 a.m., I start for Haleakala crater, and I am driving away from the town of Kahului, passing cars of many workers driving to their town jobs. Few cars are going my way. I am looking for a sign to the crater, and yes, here it is, Haleakala Crater. I am driving along on a good, paved road that begins to go gradually upward. Elevation signs at 500-foot height intervals tell me how far I have climbed. Up, up, up, gradually, through sugar cane fields, vast sugar cane on the gentle slopes of Haleakala. Now another elevation sign, and another, and finally the sugar cane fields are left behind and I am in cattle grazing country. Signs warn me to look out for cattle crossing the road.

This is a vast grazing area on the slopes of Haleakala, but I see few cattle. Where are the cattle in this Scottish-resembling land? Here and there are tall, straw-colored grass stalks and low olive-green leafy tall trees, and here and there are small groves of tall black-green leafy trees. Such vast, sweeping land! Black lava rocks speckled with green moss are on this Scottish-resembling grazing land, and I know these rocks have been thrown down from the top of the mountain.

Up, up, up I go, always up, and now the slope is steeper. An elevation sign says I am at 4500 feet. Up, up, up I go, slowly curving now. The bright blue sky and sun shining tell me this is a perfect day for the climb upward. At 5000 feet, I enter Haleakala National Park and the road is very curvy now. Slowly up, up, up. Where is the top?

At 7030 feet, I am at the Visitor's Center, and I stop my little blue Nissan to put on a sweater to counter cool air, which is not as cool as I had expected. A sign says 'do not feed the gene'. I do not see these birds. They are birds, aren't they?

I enter the Visitor's Center to take a brochure explaining about the park. Reading this gives me a chance to take a breather before returning to my little blue Nissan to continue upward. Again I am looking for gene but I do not see any. I see partridge. Maybe they are gene.

Slowly upward. Ten more miles to go. I am thinking of the height, expecting shortness of breath and a headache, but I have neither.

Now the tree line is below me and my scenery is volcanic rock. Rock, rock, rock. Dark, porous-looking lava rock, and I am looking for the silversword plant growing here amid the dark porous rock. The brochure mentions the silversword plant, but I do not see any. Where is the top?

One more mile to go. Where is the top! Less than a mile. Where! Yes, <u>finally</u>, a sign points to the crater's edge and I am driving into a parking lot and parking, glad to be here at last! I am at 9745 feet.

The view is worth the drive up, although it is cold and windy. I need a jacket and scarf over my sweater and I have neither.

I am standing at the crater's edge looking down at the moon. Twenty-two miles of a crater that looks like the moon. Dead lava cones with flat centers, like miniature mountains and craters. Spectacular, lifeless, twenty-two mile view of dead miniature mountains and craters on a dead sea of dark ash of many colors. Dark reds, dark mud colors. Awesome sight! Beautiful, awful, dead, strange. Never have I seen such a sight!

I am looking at this strange crater and suddenly I am seeing little tuffs of white clouds coming up from below, coming to the edge of the crater. Clouds coming! Time to go back!

But first I will drive just a bit further upward to the summit of this mighty Haleakala, and I am driving upward to the red lava ash parking lot at the summit. Here are four silversword plants, two with blossoms, all four with bright silver-colored, sword-shaped leaves, and I am standing in the bright clear cold air looking at these strange, majestic plants, so beautiful with their silver-colored leaves, the red ash of the summit as their home. Five to twenty-year growth and then they blossom just one time and die. Many, many seeds come from each plant and these drop onto the red ash to catch hold and spring forth. A relative of the sunflower plant. Strange.

I am climbing on foot upward to the building at the top, 10,023 feet, top of the world, and I am standing at the top of the world looking out at the majestic view of the crater. Dead land, twenty-two miles of dead land, silversword growing in the parking lot just below me, this summit a bright rust-colored ash, and then I am looking to the right of the crater at the black, iron, majestic, peaked cone thrown up by the mountain, this majestic cone interfering with compasses, I am told.

I am turning to my left to look again into the crater, and then more to my left to look out across the blue, blue sea far below me. There is Molokai Island, and a bit more left is Lanai. Now I see the big island of Hawaii where there are two volcanoes 80 and 100 miles away. Clear sky today, <u>but</u>, the clouds are coming up from below, curling over the edge of the crater just ever so little. Better to go down now.

I am starting my descent, a scare, with the feeling that one will drive off the edge and into the clouds below, but when I become used to driving downward, I feel comfortable and I am going along slowly, down, down, down, slowly, coming to 7030 feet, the Visitor's Center, not stopping, down, down, down, some cars coming up with headlights on. I am in the clouds now, not heavy clouds, down, down to the Scottish landscape, down, down through cattle country, down, down. Look at the beautiful view below! The green mountain goes down to the blue Pacific. Beautiful!

I am seeing agriculture along these slopes -- that would be the sugar cane fields -- and I am seeing the town of Kahului at the edge of the blue ocean. Yes, I am following the road down through the agriculture and to the town of Kahului and to the water's edge, to my hotel.

I am in my hotel room for noon meditation, full moon day, and I am placing in my hand the lava rock from Iao Needle, that great acupuncture needle, and I am magnetizing this rock. This meditation is for Mother Earth. Yes, for Mother Earth. Her core.

My attention is now on the House of the Sun, this Haleakala Mountain here in the middle of the great sea called Pacific, and I am making this House of the Sun <u>big</u>. Big Light. Our sun is helping, our sun knowing Haleakala Crater. Big Light coming in to activate this place. Such big Light!

At noon, the Light of the sun Alcyones of the Pleiades joins the Light of our sun, coming down to this place at Maui called Haleakala Crater, House of the Sun, Iao Needle, helping, and then down to the center of the earth, to the core, for Mother Earth. Big Light for the core. Now I am spreading this Light out across the Pacific, the entire Pacific, out, out, out, stretching this Light out to reach all the lands. Big meditation!

Today I drive to Hana at the end of the island, this place where Charles Lindbergh spent in solitude his final days. I am thinking that the adulation given to Lindbergh may have encouraged him to live isolated, in peace and quiet. Hence, Hana. I want to see the vibrations of this place. Are they similar to those in Kauai? Do they have the legacy of the love vibrations of the Lemurians?

7:30 a.m., I buy gas, clean bugs from my windshield, and I am ready for the Hana Highway, as it is called. Fifty-two miles to Hana, says the guidebook. At first the road is good, smooth, fast, sugar cane fields on either side, many cars with day workers coming to Kahului, only a few cars going my way, and <u>then</u>, a road sign says '30 miles winding road'. The road narrows and my little blue Nissan begins winding with the road. There is so much winding! I begin feeling a bit seasick, and this amuses me as I am never car sick. I think it is caused by tension. This is the worst, most dangerous road I have ever driven. <u>So</u> <u>dangerous</u>. Signs continually warn me to go 15 mph. How can one go faster? And then a 10 mph sign warning of a narrow, one-lane bridge and the need to yield to oncoming traffic. More bridges, and more. Why are there so many bridges?

This road is at the coast but one cannot see the water, only the cliff beside the road, my car nearly scraping the cliff to keep away from oncoming traffic. Fortunately, there is little oncoming traffic, and even more fortunately, there are few oncoming large cars or trucks.

I am in a tropical rain forest. Fruit, mostly red, is squashed on the road, having fallen from overhanging cliffside trees. Big ferns here. Beautiful, this place.

The sun is bright and shining and the sky is clear blue, a gorgeous day for driving even though the sun and shadows on the road are hazardous. I think this is better than rain or fog. How could one drive this road in fog? I shudder at the thought.

Onward I go, curving, winding, 15 mph, 10 mph at one-lane bridges. Tiring! When I reach Kaumahina State Park, I stop for a moment to rest and stretch my legs. A family has built a fire in one of the picnic grills, preparing breakfast. I walk behind them to see the blue, blue ocean and a stretch of tropical cliffside where I will soon be driving. So beautiful this tropical scenery, but oh, what a road!

I am driving again, going a short distance to the turnoff to the town of Keanae, and I am going slowly down a bumpy road to the water's edge, the shoreline black with lava rocks, the white spray of water splashing on these rocks. Fishermen are on the black rocks, white spray splashing on them. Beyond is the sea, so deep blue in color. A remote, beautiful place.

I see few people. Pure Hawaiian stock here, says the guidebook. Well, whoever they are, they live surrounded by beautiful scenery.

Onward now, winding, winding, winding, how much further? Where is Hana? I need to reach Hana.

Yes, finally, I reach Hana, a pretty little town spread out among flowers, shrubs, green grass, tiny neat bungalows. Tropical, comfortable living. I am thinking of Charles Lindbergh, and yes, if he liked solitude, Hana would be a wonderful place for him. But, who would want to drive fifty plus miles for supplies?

At the bay, I take off my shoes and walk along the black sandy beach, the sand feeling good between my toes. It has been hot in the car! This bay is so beautiful with its black sand and deep, deep, blue water. A fisherman is anchored offshore working on the motor of his small boat. At the far end of the bay is a long boat ramp, empty, and I walk to it and look out at the deep blue sea in this remote place. Yes, I can see why Lindbergh loved Hana, but <u>oh</u>, the road!

The vibrations here are different from Kauai. I do not feel the Lemurians here. If it were possible, and it is not, the vibrations here are older. What am I trying to say? The vibrations feel untouched by anyone or anything. The land feels free of footsteps. Later, when I am in Antarctica, the feeling is the same. It feels as if Man has not walked on this land. And yet, people live here. Charles Lindbergh lived here. I am standing here on this black sandy beach and understanding why he liked this place so much. Pure solitude.

It is time for me to leave Hana, to tackle the daunting road, but I will sidestep that task for a moment and visit Helani Gardens at the edge of Hana. At the entrance booth to the gardens, I talk with an Hawaiian woman selling tickets, a stubby yellow school bus parked beside her booth. She tells me she drives the school children to Hana from the other side of the island. She says no one else will do it, and I am understanding why! I am thinking of her driving every school day on that awful road!

I enter the gardens, no one here, and I am stopping the car and walking to a small pond of carp, big yellow, orange, orange/black, white carp, and I am talking to them and they are happy to see me. One is jumping and splashing for attention. Fun! Now I am driving along the narrow roads of the garden, every road with a different name, such as Main Drag, Garden Drive, and I am driving slowly and reading signs, 'Taxes Cause Graft', 'Evil takes hold if the Good stands aside and does nothing'. Strange to find these signs in this remote garden paradise.

Sugar cane begins to grow tall along this narrow, narrow road, and I think it is time to turn around. But the road is too narrow to turn around. I continue slowly, feeling I am lost, knowing I am lost, but the road is too narrow to turn around. I reach Link Road, and I turn on Link Road. Yes, it links to another road, and I take this road in the direction I have come. Yes, there is the workman's cottage I have seen earlier, and now I know where I am. Good. I have seen enough. I drive out of the garden, waving good-bye to the Hawaiian woman as I pass her booth, but she stops me, a yellow map in her hand. She gives me the garden map as she apologizes for having forgotten to give it to me earlier. I do not tell her I have been a bit lost.

Now I need to face fifty-two miles of tortuous road, and I am settling in to start the grueling drive, but, what is this? A little red car is just ahead of me and the driver is a good driver. He knows the road. I follow him the entire distance, almost mesmerized by the little red car expertly tackling the road ahead of me. Such a help to follow it! The driver is taking all the worries of the blind curves, one-lane bridges, etc., and I am following his little red car all the way, until he turns off just before Kalului to climb Haleakala Mountain. He will take that road to the top? To the crater? Just after the Hana road? Well, sir, you have a lot of stamina! I return to my hotel, take a big swim in the pool, eat lunch in my room, then a rest until meditating at 4:15 p.m.

This meditation is big, very big. As I am meditating, the sun breaks through the clouds, bursts into my room, shines on me. I am thinking of the House of the Sun, Haleakala, and I am combining the vibrations/ energies of this place with the sun shining on me, then showering the combined energies onto all of Maui. Big, big Light is coming in. Bigger than yesterday.

This island called Maui, home of Haleakala, House of the Sun, is male. The big island of Hawaii is female, guarded by Maui. I am thinking on the Island of the Sun, male, at Lake Titicaca, whose mate, the female island, is sleeping. Here, the big island called Hawaii, the female, is awakened, and this creates a possibility of blending the two Lights, male/female, Maui/ big island of Hawaii, equal/equal for the benefit of the Pacific lands, for the benefit of the Ring of Fire, for the benefit of Mother Earth.

This morning I am driving to Lahaina, a clean, prosperous town with many tourist shops, this being a place for tourists to see where, in the old days, fifty whaling ships could be moored, says the guidebook. I am parking the Nissan beside a row of seaside tourist shops and walking on a long causeway to reach the old whaling port. I see a small white-painted lighthouse. Not adequate, I think, but who am I to comment on the adequacy of lighthouses? In front of the lighthouse is moored an old whaling ship with tall sails, the Carthaginian, now serving as a museum.

Further out are many tourists on a bright red, gaily-painted, old ship. This is a bright sunny day for the tourists to be enjoying the sights of this place, and I am walking along and looking at all the little sailboats and pleasure cruisers moored here. The place is jammed packed with pleasure boats!

I am turning my attention to the Pioneer Inn just in front of the harbor, a green and white painted building with an orange roof and a second-floor verandah circling the inn. I am entering and walking upstairs to this verandah, seating myself in a chair overlooking the ocean, looking out at the sea just as the whaling captains did in the old days. This inn is a wonderful, grand old place reminding me of Somerset Maugham and the Sadie Thompson stories. Seated on the verandah near me are two young men wearing spectacles primly looking out. On the old days when the port was active with whaling ships, certainly there would be missionaries here. These two sitting on the verandah would fit in perfectly during the days of looking out at a sinful world.

I am leaving the verandah and walking to a banyan tree beside the Pioneer Inn, this mighty old tree taking up space the size of a playground, and I am thinking what tales this banyan tree could relate! I am looking at this mighty old tree, its branches so thick and heavy and spread out so far, it would seem impossible for them not to break, but no, this has not happened. Care has been taken. Here and there, from the ground to the branches, are poles holding the hefty weight. Sturdy rubber straps hold the poles and branches in place. I am walking around the tree, looking at the leaves, looking at the main trunk in the center, looking at the other trunks, many other trunks encouraged to grow from the ground to the branches, or maybe it is from the branches to the ground. I do not know. Never have I seen a tree like this one!

Now I am driving up the coast toward expensive hotels planted seaside, and I am driving through acres of green, well-maintained grass and palm trees, coming to the Hyatt Regent Maui Hotel. My guidebook says this is an eighty million dollar, 20-acre complex with lush waterfalls and gardens. I am parking my car and walking into this complex, studying a colored chart, speaking to a talking gray African parrot perched at a nearby window, then entering Japanese-style, well-maintained gardens of green grass, palm trees, shrubs, little shrines, pools of orange, white, black carp, and yes, pink flamingos. I have never seen pink flamingos, but these must be pink flamingos.

I am walking to a huge swimming pool, this one stretching to miniature falls, and then the pool continues under the falls to a regular-sized swimming pool. So <u>elegant</u>. All this within a grassy area running parallel to a sandy beach where people are sunbathing and some are swimming in the ocean.

I absorb the beauty around me, and then I retrace my steps, walking through the Japanese garden, seeing again the pink flamingos, talking again to the parrot, he reminding me of the talking parrot in Africa that chewed my shoe. Inside the hotel complex, I see a lone penguin snoozing at its tiny pond. A bright colored parrot is perched in the atrium, not caged, not leashed, eating a large nut with slow, deliberate bites. Such a magnificent hotel!

CHAPTER 4

The Big Island of Hawaii, Pele's Home

This morning before flying from Maui to Hilo on the big island of Hawaii, I lean on the second flood railing of the open walkway of my hotel to look one last time at the green grass below, the swimming pool, palm trees, small beach, and the tall, green mountains far away. It is cloudy today and there is haze on these mountains. A hotel maid has told me she is unhappy with the haze because she likes the sunshine. She says the haze is coming from a volcanic eruption yesterday on the big island of Hawaii, and there have been eruptions for over two months. I am surprised. I have known nothing about these eruptions.

Now I am driving to the airport to take an Air Hawaiian plane, a 4-motor plane with wings overhead. My seat is just under the wing area, my view somewhat limited, but it is fun to take this type of plane, smooth, not noisy, carrying about 100 passengers. Almost all seats are taken. A beefy Hawaiian sitting beside me is careful not to nudge me with his big arms. I am drinking with a straw tropical fruit punch from a small box as we are flying along, and I am looking out the window as the pilot in a folksy manner is describing Maui sights below. I see the slopes of Haleakala, then the coastline to Hana, and Hana itself. I am taking one last look at the bay of Hana, such a beautiful place, and I am thinking of Lindbergh who liked the solitude of living there.

Now we are crossing the blue Pacific, and soon we are approaching the big island of Hawaii. Heavy white clouds greet us and we plunge into them, flying blindly for a moment before clear sky takes charge. I am looking at the gentle slopes of a mountain, probably Mauna Kea, its cultivated slopes gently going to the water. Neat patches of various colors and shades distinguish different crops. The pilot begins telling us about the huge Parker cattle ranch below, and how the ranch started with two acres given to a Massachusetts man named Parker by the ruling Hawaiian king who wanted to rid the island of goats and pigs devastating the island's vegetation. Didn't I earlier hear another reason why the Parker ranch was started? Well, never mind.

We are coming down now, landing at Hilo airport, a pretty little place, its terminal interior resembling a garden. I pick up tourist brochures and road maps and a little red Nissan with air conditioning, and away I go to Hilo Hukilau Hotel, my home for the next few days. My room overlooks a large tropical fish pond, and I am looking down at orange, white, black carp, and little Japanese-style humped bridges crossing the pond to connect to tiny islands with small Japanese shrines. A big banyan tree spreads its branches over one edge of the pond.

A finger of Hilo Bay is close to my hotel, and here I see an attractive restaurant with people dining inside at little tables, seated at windows.

I am looking at this beautiful scenery, and I am especially looking at the carp lazily swimming a few feet below me. One white carp, three-quarters grown, is particularly interested in the water surface. Is he hunting for bugs? Two mallards, a male and a female, are sleeping on a tiny island in the center of this pond. What fun to see all this! What beauty!

I put on my swim suit and head for the open air pool in the inner part of the hotel. A long, lazy swim is needed! It is like swimming in Paradise.

This afternoon I intend to drive to Rainbow Falls, a short distance outside Hilo, and now I am leaving my hotel and driving parallel to the bay on Kamehameha Avenue, going along slowly, looking at all the green, so much green. Usually a city is full of buildings with a bit of green around the buildings, but this place, Hilo, seems to be green with a bit of buildings. I am going along through all this green, and because it is Saturday afternoon, I see Hawaiians in family groups picnicking and playing sports. I am coming to a stoplight complex and a row of buildings for small businesses, and here I make a mistake by taking Route 19 out of Hilo, going upward along gentle cultivated mountain slopes. I am thinking, no, this direction is not right, and I am turning around, returning to the row of small business buildings, going behind these buildings, climbing a bit, and yes, here is the road, Waianuenue Avenue, and yes, there is the sign to Rainbow Falls. I am going along a bit through a residential area, and, oh dear, another wrong turn, but what a huge banyan tree! I am slowing to look at this huge banyan tree, then turning around, retracing my way a bit, and yes, here is Rainbow Falls.

I stop to look at two waterfalls, not large, plunging into a deep green pool, and then the water in the form of a river continues to the Pacific. This area here is lush green with vegetation.

After a good look at the falls, I continue toward a place called Boiling Pots, wanting to see these boiling pots, volcanic boiling pots. But, where are they? I am looking down at a turbulent river, looking here and there, scanning for boiling pots, and I do not see them. Where are they? Is the Hawaiian meaning different from my meaning? Turbulence riles the water into the shapes of pools/pots. Maybe there are no volcanic boiling pots. I am disappointed.

I return to Hilo to buy food. Sparkling, carbonated water from Napa Valley, cheese, grapes, bread, lettuce, bananas, yogurt. My room has a refrigerator but no air conditioning. A room sign asks guests to conserve on electricity which costs five times more than on the Mainland. I am thinking, there is no shortage of water, and so hydroelectric power should be cheap. Why is it not being used?

I eat an early supper looking out at the fish pond, watching the orange, black, white carp swimming just below me. A pair of ducks are lazily paddling side by side. Very pleasant here. It begins to rain, heavy rain coming down hard onto the fish pond, making big splats on the water, and the orange, black, white carp are swimming here and there investigating the big splats, looking for bugs falling from overhanging tree branches. So much fun watching all this. And yes, so much rain! Seven inches maybe. But warm, pleasant.

I phone my mother this morning to wish her a happy birthday and I am reaching her easily. It is 6:30 a.m. on a Sunday morning here in Hawaii, and 12:30 p.m. where she lives. At 7:30 a.m. I am in my little red Nissan headed to Hawaii Volcanoes National Park on Highway 11, a fast, good road with no traffic this early Sunday morning. Just outside Hilo, lush rain forest scenery greets me. The road is going gently upward, 500 feet above sea level, 1000 feet, up, up, gently, and I am looking at tropical trees and big ferns. Some squashed red fruit is on the road. At 4000 feet the trees change to a spindly, long-branched type and there are tree skeletons. Has this area been burned?

The road is good all the way and very quickly I am at Hawaii Volcanoes National Park, only a twenty-two mile drive from Hilo. I stop at the Visitor's Center and Park Headquarters, and I soon have with me a map of the route to take around the Kilauea Crater rim just ahead. A movie will be showing at the Visitor's Center in twenty minutes. Should I see the movie before circling the crater? I ask a park woman, who, without hesitation, tells me not to wait for the movie. I must go immediately to see the crater because heavy clouds are coming and the weather can change abruptly. And so, although I am disappointed not to see the movie, I am heeding her advice and leaving the Visitor's Center to begin my trip around the crater.

I have not yet seen any evidence of the crater, and there has been no indication that I am actually at the summit of this active Kilauea volcano considered by the Hawaiians to be the most active volcano in the world. I go along a bit, and when my map says to turn off the road to see steam vents, I do this, and suddenly I am at a big scorched place. A strong smell of rotten eggs is coming from steam rising out of the ground. I am stopping and getting out of my car and standing at this place, looking at the steam rising out of the ground. Just beyond is a place of no vegetation, and yet, I see evidence of ferns beginning to think about returning. Steam vents and foliage are living side by side here. I am looking north, south, east, west, and yes, steam vents are everywhere. Strange to see steam coming out of the ground. Unsettling. I begin to think I am standing on a steam vent.

I drive a bit further along the crater rim road, and there are more vents. Openings in the ground letting out steam. Strange. A sign points to a crater rim overlook, and I am stopping and walking to the rim and looking down. Good grief!!!! Huge crater! Round. Black crust. One end of the crater has a large, depressed, round section deeper than the main section. Never have I seen such a sight! Shocking! Ghastly! I am asking, why is this awful place here with everything dead? For relieving tension, I am given the thought. And so I understand that it is necessary. Awful, awesome sight. Burned death of the earth.

I am driving further, following the rim of this Kilauea Crater, eleven miles around, stopping at signs to read, 'Here was the site of the 1974 eruption', 'here 1969', 'here 1971'. This place has great fissures of black, burned, porous, cracked, uplifted lava making strange black patterns. I stop to walk on this black, cracked lava. Crunch, crunch, crunch. My shoes are making black cinders. Everything is burned, dead.

At the Halemaumau overlook, such a strong smell of sulfur! Signs warning people with heart and lung problems to not linger. I am getting out of my car here and walking crunch, crunch, crunch over porous, black lava that turns to black cinders underfoot, smelling the sulfur, looking at the steam vents, many steam vents here, little shrines and offerings to appease Pele, home of the goddess. One little offering on the black lava is a fish. Another is a ripe papaya and another is a small bottle of gin. Obviously, some think Pele likes gin.

I am walking over the black lava at the rim of the crater, Halemaumau Crater, home of Pele, Goddess of Fire, and at the very edge of the crater, on the other side of the guard rail, are more offerings to Pele. Incense sticks burning, cloth strip with Japanese writing, a little, circular offering of flowers arranged around a cluster of lava.

I am looking down now over the rim and into the crater, sunken, black, lifeless, awful, home of Pele. Oh dear, I would have preferred a nicer home.

I continue driving along the Crater Rim Road, as it is called, looking at the black, dead land where outpourings from the crater have scorched the land, so much land black and broken.

Terrible, and yet, here and there begins a fern and a beginning of a clump of grass. The beginnings.

I am watching the time, knowing the movie at the Visitor's Center begins on the hour, and I am driving faster now, not stopping at Devastation Trail or the Lava Tube, going quickly through a fern forest, not everything has been destroyed here at Pele's home, and yes, I am arriving at the Visitor's Center at five minutes to ten.

The movie is well worth seeing, for it describes how the magma comes up from the core and fills the center of a mountain and then the lava finds cracks on the slopes that bring it to the surface. This has been happening on this island for over two months. The new eruption is quite far from Kilauea Crater, in dense forest that cannot be reached by car. Rangers discovered the eruption when they searched to put out a fire thought to be started by lightning.

The movie dramatically shows the 1974 eruption. A great force of red lava comes out of the earth and pours down a mountain slope like a rushing river, down through the forests, burning the trees, burning everything in its way, finally reaching the sea, hitting the sea with a mighty splash and a great plum of steam rises from this fierce contact with the sea. Yes, the movie is dramatic.

After the movie, I tour the lava displays at the Visitor's Center, and I see different types of lava and different types of minerals brought up from the depths of the earth by the eruptions. During my drive around the crater's rim, when I have seen tiny ferns and bits of grass that have caught hold on the black, scorched land, I did not realize that the minerals brought up from the depths are food for the plants. Out of death comes life. Yes, I am remembering the little ferns and grass and I am saying in telepathy to them, 'Keep at it. Keep growing. Bring in your brothers and sisters.' Yes, there is life even after such awful destruction.

I am leaving the Visitor's Center and walking across the street to the Volcano House, a hotel, and yes, the scenery is beautiful here. There is a bit of rain forest landscape and even a vent. If I ever come to this island again, I will try to stay one night here. I am entering the hotel, and what is this? A view of the crater? The hotel is directly on the rim of the crater? I am standing at a plate glass window looking at the fantastic view!

It is time to look at other views and I am going to Thurston Lava Tube to take an interesting walk through the rain forest to enter a tube-like, natural earth formation, which, I assume has been the result of an eruption. The strange formations of this burned land are becoming more attractive as I begin to understand the functioning, the importance of the great lava flows coming from the bowels of the earth.

Now I am driving down Chain of Crater Road to reach the sea, and I am going mile after mile down toward the sea through black land, mile after mile of black lava that has poured out of the crater and down to the sea, smothering everything in its path. Yes, this path of black lava is extensive. Not just one thin finger of lava but a very, very wide path. I can feel the force of the destruction!

At the ocean, I see the black cliff coast line, not a high cliff coast line, but nevertheless a cliff. I am stopping at one place to see a natural black lava arch hanging from the cliff and going down into the deep blue-purple water. I drive mile after mile on the sea road, no habitation here, no, not after such destruction, and finally I stop at an old heiau, a sacred place with remains of black lava walls. But I am not staying long. No. The former practice of human sacrifice sends me away. I do not like the vibrations here.

Finally, the road goes along the black lava, green vegetation coast, and a bit farther, just before Kaimu, begins black sandy beaches. Hawaiians are on these beaches. I see four colorfully painted native outriggers, a skinny type of boat. I am close to the airport now, my thoughts on my hotel just ahead. Yes, it is time for a swim in the pool followed by a late lunch.

During my 4:30 p.m. meditation, I work with the entire island, this female island. Yes, so female, this island. A nice island. Pleasant. No wrath here, which is a bit surprising considering the presence of an active volcano.

I am joining this island, female, with the male/Maui, Island of the Sun.

The Old Man and his Hawaiian Garden:

This morning my destination is Akaka Falls State Park. The sun is bright, sky blue, temperature comfortable as I am driving on a gentle mountain slope of sugar cane fields. Then I turn off the main road to take a scenic route close to the sea through a rain forest. I am driving slowly, looking at huge tropical trees, some red fruit droppings on the road, and I am running over this squashed fruit as well as twigs, branches, leaves. This road is not heavily traveled. I am going along through this rain forest, admiring the scenery, but not seeing the sea, and then suddenly I am out of the rain forest and here is the coast with its black, black lava cliffs bordering the deep blue sea. Beautiful!

I am approaching Akaka Falls State Park, entering the park, my thoughts on the falls. Yes, that will be my first stop this morning. I am parking and immediately spotting a trail leading down into the rain forest, and I am starting down this rain forest path, alone, and I am thinking it is early and there is no one here. Is this wise? Then I am hearing someone on the path above me, and I am turning and seeing an old man in his eighties coming down the path, machete in his hand, whacking a leaf too close to the path, using the point of his machete to poke away a fallen branch. I am calling up to him, asking if he is the gardener, and he is calling down that he has built this trail.

Thus it begins, one and one half hours with this old man, he telling me stories of plants brought here from far off lands like Guam, Siam, and India. Many places. He says he started building this place in 1935 and now he is retired and is working as a volunteer because he cannot let go. We talk and talk about his garden and his past, and he is telling me he is of Portuguese descent, his father having come from Portugal bringing a seed which his father has planted here. This seed turned into a tree, a type unknown to park rangers, and they had to research two months before discovering the name of the tree. The man is standing here in his garden telling me all this, saying his father kept a diary now under lock and key in a museum and when he wants to see his father's diary, he has to register.

We are talking and talking and now we are looking at a <u>huge</u> red flower, a type of ginger flower dangling beside the path still attached to its stalk. The old man is saying probably a tourist has tried to take it and has not succeeded, and so this huge, gorgeous flower is left dangling on the path. The man with one swipe of his sharp machete is cutting off the huge red flower and handing it to me, explaining that the stalk is a solid mass of fibers and no one is strong enough to twist it off. The tourist has not known this.

We are standing on the path the old man has made for the tourists, looking at the huge red flower and the old man is telling me to take it home. I am looking at this beautiful specimen of Nature and saying no, the customs people will not allow me to take it onto the Mainland. I am also thinking it would be terrible to take this gorgeous flower with me because it will die and I do not want to see this flower dying. We two are standing together in this rain forest, his garden, looking at this beautiful flower, we needing to make a decision, and the old man is saying we have two choices, either I take it with me or we throw it down the slope where it will be hidden from view and allowed to go back to the earth and be recycled. I choose the latter, and so we have looked at this beautiful red flower of Nature for the last time and the old man has thrown it into the rain forest, hidden forever from view, allowed to go back into the earth in peace. This has been a solemn ritual for both of us.

We are walking a bit further along his garden path through the rain forest and he is showing me clumps of Guam bamboo he has planted. Huge clumps of slim-stalked bamboo, and he is pointing out one very large bamboo stalk from Siam, fallen, dead. This type, he tells me, lives only seven years, and I am looking at this huge, single, fallen bamboo, the size the river people on the Li River in China use to make their boats. Three or four of these bamboo stalks lashed together make a sturdy boat.

Now we come to Kahuna Falls, which I did not even know was here, and we are looking at the falls located across a ravine. The old man points to a TV satellite dish above the falls, and I am looking at this satellite dish almost hidden by trees as he tells me that just above the falls, near the satellite, is a house. Yes, I see it. And the old man is saying it belongs to a retired pilot who swims every morning in a pool just before the drop for the falls. The old man and I are standing in the rain forest looking at the pool on the other side of the ravine, and the old man is saying it is dangerous swimming there. One slip and the pilot will go over the falls. I do not comment but I am thinking it is not really that dangerous. We two, the old man and I, are thinking about the retired pilot who has come out here and built his house so far away from everyone and who swims daily in the pool above the falls. Well, why not. Lindbergh found his little paradise in remote Hana.

The old man is picking two white ginger flowers, two different types, and the smell of the white ginger is wonderful. So <u>fragrant</u>. I am putting the two blossoms in my hair like Hawaiian girls do, and the old man and I are walking along the path he has made many years ago, and he is showing me blue ginger and yellow ginger and red ginger. Then I look up and see high in a tree an orchid, its white roots coming down the tree branches to the trunk. I ask how he has put that orchid up there and he tells me he has climbed up to plant it. With his machete, he points to orchids planted high up in several trees.

A man is approaching, a tourist, and the old man says they walk along the path never looking up to see the orchids. I stop this tourist to tell him to look up to see the orchids and he pauses, looks up, and walks on without a change of expression. Yes, I understand the old man's comments about the tourists who come to his garden.

But some tourists are responsive. Now we are joined by a couple from San Francisco who, when the old man points out a blue ginger he has planted far back from the path so tourists cannot pick the blossoms, are thrilled to see the blue ginger and they join us. The old man is pointing here and there to his plants and telling the names and we are asking questions and another couple joins us. They, too, are interested in the plants, and the woman is saying she recently has become interested in plants because she has baby sat for them in other people's homes. Now, when she enters a house, she always notices the plants.

The old man is showing us a special plant with beautiful flowers he has planted behind a big bush so the tourists will not pick the flowers, and we are looking at this special plant. I am thinking of the people who pick his flowers. He is saying the Hawaiian girls take all his gardenia flowers for their hair, and some people not only pick his flowers but they also steal his plants. So much fun talking with this old man!

He is showing us red bananas and lobster claw flowering trees and a beef heart flowering tree and now he is saying he has a vegetable garden at home with tomatoes and celery and more. Because he has an excess of beans, he has tried to give them to his dentist and grocer, but his grocer is overstocked.

We are approaching Akaka Falls and we are looking at it just as a rainbow appears across the lower part of the falls. The old man says it will stay two hours because of the position of the sun. I am amazed! Mother Nature has given humanity a beautiful sight. In the old days, says the old man, Hawaiians used to live at the bottom of the falls, and there is evidence today of trees they cultivated for food. Many Hawaiians are buried here because this is a special place. I am looking at the falls with the rainbow and thinking of the Hawaiians who used to live in this Paradise years and years ago.

Now the old man is pointing to a row of fifty or more eucalyptus trees high up on the ridge, and he is saying he and his brother planted these tall, stately trees many, many years ago. He also tells us about the time he and his brother gathered bananas high up on the ridge, and they had picked and picked and picked until they had so many, they had a terrible time carrying them home. Tales of the old days. So much fun hearing his stories!

He tells us about the wild pigs that dig into the earth to eat worms and this disturbs the ecology of the place. And he tells us of his introduction of the philodendron plant here in his garden, a terrible mistake because its iron grip has taken hold of trees, strangling them. We are walking along and seeing huge philodendron vines strangling trees, and we are seeing attempts by the old man's machete to cut the vines at the base of the trees, but it is no use. I am thinking of the philodendron in the window of my house. Such an innocent little plant. It is not strangling anything.

The old man stops at a little brook with overhanging, gigantic green ferns, and as we are looking down at this beautiful sight, he points out a rectangular, cleared place in the pool. This rectangular place has only recently appeared, he tells us, and he thinks is it an ancient grave. This is a sacred pool, he says, and I agree.

I am thinking of this old man in his eighties, caretaker of this sacred land, his sacred rain forest garden, and he is hacking here and there with his machete to keep the path clear. It is an endless task, yet, this caretaker of this sacred place loves it. <u>Such an experience to meet this wonderful old man</u>! Lemurian Love, that is what this man is giving Nature. A legacy of the past.

Now we are at the top of his garden and he is showing me a Kona coffee plant and then a Monostro Delicioso tree with long, eight-to-ten inch green fruit. He is hunting here and there for a ripe one. Yes, here is one, and he is cutting it off with his machete, then using his pocket knife to peel away the outside, cutting off small pieces and handing them for me to eat. The inside looks like an overripe banana combined with a pineapple look. So <u>delicious</u> is the taste! He is giving me more. <u>Delicious</u>. What fun!

I am reluctant to leave this wonderful old man and his love for his wonderful garden that returns his love. Shades of Lemuria. I drive away with my thoughts are on him and his garden, knowing I have just been blessed with a beautiful experience.

I drive north, up the coast, and the land is sugar cane country, the cane being harvested. Many big trucks are on the road carrying the cane away from the fields. One field of harvested sugar cane is being burned.

I am looking for cattle country, and yes, now, as I am driving inland to green pastoral elevated land with few trees, some eucalyptus, I see brown and white cattle behind fences. To my left, lost in the clouds, is the top of Mauna Kea, a huge mountain, its gentle slopes going down 13,796 feet to sea level and then thousands and thousands of feet under the water. To my right are the heavily forested Kohala Mountains.

I stop at Waimea, a small, prosperous-looking town in the heart of cattle country to buy post cards at the Parker Ranch Shopping Center. Didn't I read that this is the largest cattle ranch in the United States, which means it is bigger than the King ranch in Texas? Cowboys still work on the Parker ranch. Well, of course they would be working on the ranch. Who else would be working on it?

The next day, 9 a.m., I drive a short way to Hilo Tropical Gardens, about a half mile from my hotel, and just as I arrive, rain comes down in torrents. I wait in my little rental car for it to subside and then I make a dash for the gift shop at the entrance to the gardens. Here I am greeted with a gift, a tiny, purple orchid, and I pin this to my blouse. In the shop I buy white ginger perfume, a fragrance I will always associate with Hawaii.

What do I hear? A busload of tourists descending on the gift shop, lining up to receive their gift of a tiny orchid So many tourists! The place is inundated with them, and here comes another busload. Oh dear! To escape them, I enter the garden of dripping wet leaves and flowers. Here they come! Now we are all walking among the dripping wet leaves and flowers and cameras are going click, click, click. What happened to peace and quiet?

I am seeing blue ginger flowers and lobster claw plants and strange flowers looking like they are made out of wax. Orchids are here, cultivated, orderly, not as sensational as yesterday's orchids in the old man's garden. For a moment I am thinking of the old man and his fascination for orchids. I am walking among the flowers and the plants here at Hilo Tropical Gardens, very wet underfoot and the leaves and flowers are dripping, and I am using my red umbrella and the tourists are using waxed Japanese parasols provided by the garden. Soon they return to their buses and the garden is quiet, peaceful. I am leaving, too, wanting to leave before more buses arrive.

I return to the hotel to meditate, and yes, this meditation is big. Strong Light is coming down, and I am joining Maui Island of the Sun with the big island of Hawaii. Afterward I am tired, TIRED, and I am lying on the bed, unable to move from the tiredness. Then the Special Ones come, and They are asking telepathically if I know They are here. Yes. They tell me I have done well.

This afternoon I am going to the Wailoa River State Park's Visitor Center a bit inland from Hilo Bay, and here I am looking at photographs of a past tsunami, a huge tidal wave that has come across the land at Hilo Bay destroying the land, buildings, killing people. I look at a photograph of a man in a small boat cutting the anchor rope of a large ship so it can escape the wave. This man is killed doing this heroic act and the ship has been saved.

Terrible, these tsunamis. One has come because of an earthquake in Chile, and it has traveled all that way in fourteen hours to overwhelm Hilo Bay. Another has come because of a quake in the Aleutians. I understand why there is so much undeveloped area at Hilo Bay. I would not want to live there.

Now I am driving parallel to Hilo Bay on Bayfront Highway, as it is called, and I am looking to my left at the black, sandy beach and at the purple-blue water. To my right is Liliukalani Gardens, an extensive green area with little fish ponds, Japanese-style bridges, and pavilions. I park and walk to a small red pavilion to watch fish jumping in a pond. Mourning doves are calling, their call different from those living at home. The Hawaiian ones look like a cross between our mourning doves and South African mourning doves.

So beautiful this place. Little walkways and curved bridges, everything so well maintained, and I am sitting at the red pavilion looking at the pond and the jumping fish. At the same time, I am looking straight ahead at Hilo Bay with its black sand and purple-blue water, thinking of the tsunami that has come here to this land that now is a beautiful Japanese garden. Also, I am looking at the gentle slopes of the land coming to the bay, a suggestion here and there of sugar cane fields being burned on this patchwork quilt of agricultural fields.

Now for a swim in the hotel pool, and that is it for the day.

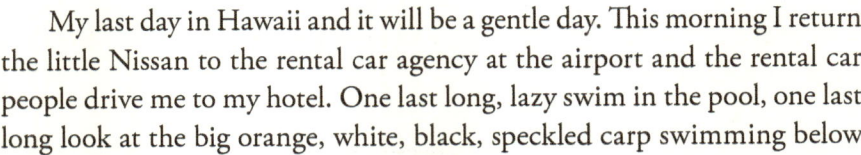

My last day in Hawaii and it will be a gentle day. This morning I return the little Nissan to the rental car agency at the airport and the rental car people drive me to my hotel. One last long, lazy swim in the pool, one last long look at the big orange, white, black, speckled carp swimming below my room. The duck pair have left. Lunch in my room, refrigerator cleaned out, and then it is time to leave my room, but not yet time to catch my plane to the Mainland, as the islanders call the 48 States.

I leave my bag at the hotel to walk along Banyan Drive, my hotel being at the beginning of this circular drive, and I am walking along this circular Banyan Drive, its name coming from banyans planted here by celebrities. Yes, here is Amelia Earhart's tree, planted January 6, 1935, and I stop for a moment to look at her tree. Strange how this big tree has such a delicate, feminine feeling to it. The other trees on the drive do not have this delicate feeling. I am looking at the George Herman 'Babe' Ruth tree, Cecil B. DeMille tree, Senator Richard Nixon tree, Doctors this and that, the Honorable somebody, and a Princess somebody who probably is part of the Hawaiian royal family. Interesting how often this royal family crops up in conversations with the Hawaiians, and I am thinking the Hawaiians would be satisfied having their royal family in power, with the benefits of being part of the United States, of course. And here is a George Marshall tree. All the trees are big with very wide trunks and big shoots paralleling the main trunk. Most have been planted during the early 1930's.

I am walking slowly along Banyan Drive, continuing along until I reach the Japanese Garden, and I am again sitting at the red pavilion looking at the fish in the pond, looking at Hilo Bay, looking at the gentle slopes coming down to the sea with their patchwork quilts of agricultural fields. I am sitting here lazily looking at everything, knowing this will be the last time I will be sitting here looking at all this.

Now it is time to leave the Big Island of Hawaii, and I walk back to the hotel and take a taxi to the airport. I am still two and one half hours early, but nevertheless, it is time to go to the airport. What? The woman at the ticket counter is saying my flight coming in from the Mainland will be delayed, fog or clouds or something, and it would be better for me to book another flight. I am agreeing and she is booking me on Aloha Airlines. What? A plane is leaving in five minutes. Do I want to be on it? Well, why not, and I rush to catch the plane to Honolulu.

I am flying now over the Big Island of Hawaii. Clouds greet us, but we are climbing high, and yes, we are out of the clouds, and yes, here is the top of Mauna Kea, her summit enjoying bright, clear sky. So peaceful this mountain, and I am looking at this place as we are flying by, saying good-bye to this peaceful mountain, a stabilizing influence for this island.

A quick flight, about twenty-eight minutes, and we are coming down at Honolulu Airport.

CHAPTER 5

Oahu, Home of Diamond Head

Earlier, flying from Kauai to Maui, I have stopped briefly at the Honolulu Airport in Oahu, and here is my account of this brief moment. We are flying over the blue Pacific, looking down at the calm water, and as we are approaching Oahu, I am noting that this island is not as green as Kauai. We are coming in low over Pearl Harbor and I am looking down curiously at this famous place, trying to locate the upside-down Arizona. Yes, that must be the monument to the ship, and I am looking at this place called Pearl Harbor, small place, inland from the coast, and I am thinking, this place was a trap. No doubt in my mind about that. I am thinking, why would anyone put a fleet in that trap? It makes no sense to me. Many have paid dearly for that mistake.

We are landing at Honolulu airport, a short hop from Pearl Harbor, stopping long enough to unload and pick up passengers before we are off again, flying across the water, paralleling the coastline. Waikiki Beach is below us and I am looking down at the skyscrapers and hotels, one right after the other. The city does not interest me.

We are flying a bit farther and the pilot is telling us we are looking at Diamond Head Mountain, and he is explaining that when sailors first saw the sparkling mountain, they thought they were seeing diamonds, but no, it was silicon glittering in the sunlight, looking like diamonds. I note that Diamond Head does not have the green of the Kauai Mountains.

The next time I visit the land called Oahu, it is evening and I am with Doreen. We are stopping at Honolulu on our way to Australia, Indonesia, Singapore, and India. When we leave the plane, we feel the warmth, gentle breeze, and balminess of Oahu. This feels good. We claim our luggage, book a room at the Continental Surf, one block inland from Waikiki Beach, a good location for us, and a taxi takes us to the hotel along dark city streets. I look at concrete forests of tall, lighted skyscrapers, and I feel this city called Honolulu has a population out of proportion to the land. When we arrive at the hotel, a concrete skyscraper, Room 2101 on the 21st floor is ready for us. We make peppermint tea in the kitchenette and then go to bed. Today has been a long journey from the eastern part of the Mainland.

We wake early, 4 a.m. local time, and decide to build a sunrise healing Agnihotra fire at the beach. Doreen is expert at making this fire. An Agnihotra pot, ghee, rice, and cow dung are necessary ingredients for building a proper Agnihotra fire, and we have these necessities in our baggage. As we step out of the hotel, ingredients in hand, warm air greets us, and a red flower growing in a hotel planter greets us. Yes, early this morning, as we are leaving the hotel, a strong feeling of Hawaii greets us.

We are walking in the dark to the sandy beach, and we are choosing a place close to the water to build the healing fire. Few are up at this early hour. We will not be disturbed. I am watching Doreen as she builds the fire, and I am talking to the elves and gnomes and fairies and elementals gathering here with us, welcoming us. I am explaining about the fire and the purification and they are waiting with great excitement for the lighting of the fire. There is a pesky breeze and Doreen is having trouble lighting the fire. They are becoming worried she will not be able to light the fire, but I assure them she will light it. We will not miss the sunrise.

Yes! The fire is lit and the smoke is smelling so good! Big energy is coming from the fire. I am surprised at so much energy and I am beginning to send the energy out to all of the Pacific. WHAT IS THIS? Hawaiian High Ones, warriors of old, are coming in. Many! These are boisterous ones. They are here at the fire and I am speaking to them, telling them about Doreen and the fire for sending energy to all the Pacific. SO SURPRISING THEY ARE HERE!!!

Dawn comes and the beach is feeling beautiful, friendly. My heart beats fast with happiness. The fire is strong, powerful! The Old Ones and the gnomes and the fairies and the elementals are here with us, witnessing this healing fire. I watch as the fire gradually turns to ash, and then Doreen puts it into the water to energize the ocean.

———◆———

New Moon Day:

This morning Doreen and I take a crowded public bus to Diamond Head crater. On this bus we worry where to get off, but our worries are needless because others want to go to Diamond Head. When it is time, about ten of us struggle to reach the door to leave. Then we begin climbing a slope, walking slowly in the heat, and when we enter the crater via a short tunnel, we reach a parking lot, picnicking area and toilet facilities. US Army trucks and other military vehicles are nearby, all inside the crater.

Doreen and I continue climbing slowly to reach the top of the crater rim, going through a dark tunnel, climbing straight up ninety-nine steps. Exhausting to climb in the heat. Finally we are at the top and we stop at a World War II gun emplacement. I sense the violation of sacred Diamond Head. I know the noise of the big guns has weighed heavily on the vibrations of this mountain. There is much need for healing. Yes, this place has not recovered from World War II, and I am thinking tourists are unintentionally prolonging the violation, some being veterans returning with memories, thinking, thinking, thinking about that time, stimulating that awful thought form of violence and death. Mother Earth here has not recovered.

The inside of the mountain has been dug out to bring up guns and ammunition, a violation of Mother Earth's guts. We feel the weakness here. No vitality in this mountain called Diamond Head, this place so important for the Pacific, and thus it is absolutely essential for this place be healed if it is to be used to send out healing energy for the whole of the Pacific.

We are sitting on the gun emplacement to look out at the blue Pacific. Just beyond the gun emplacement is a sharp drop and far below is tropical green vegetation, some houses.

It is not possible for Doreen to build a fire here, but we can meditate. We are worrying that tourists will come, maybe some ex-soldiers with their conversations and thoughts of war, but, just before 12 noon, a quiet descends on this place and we are alone. At 12 noon a big Light comes, healing Light, and I am taking it to the center of this mountain, using the sun's energy of 12 noon to stimulate the glittering silicon. We are working very hard here to heal the mountain.

Afterwards, we feed a persistent, tame pigeon and two mourning doves pieces of sugar coffee cake sprinkled with healing ash before beginning our walk downward, down the ninety-nine steps, through the long tunnel that has violated the interior of the mountain, to the center of the crater. It is beginning to rain, a warm rain, and I am using my red umbrella as we are walking in the center of the crater to the picnic area to eat lunch at a table and feed bright, red-crested, black and white jays or cardinals or whatever they are.

After lunch, we leave the crater via the small tunnel, walking down the slope of the mountain, and at the road we are looking for the bus stop just as a taxi comes, stops, and offers us a special rate to take us back to the beach. We are accepting. Thank you, Higher Worlds! We are tired!

The taxi driver takes us to the posh Hyatt Regency Hotel where we have stored our luggage after checking out of our hotel. We are entering this posh Hyatt Regency Hotel filled with Japanese, and we are sitting beside a waterfall in a large open-interior patio, ordering ice tea that comes with a sugar cane stick, pineapple chunk, lemon slice, and a small white orchid which I put in a button hole of my blouse. But the orchid is in danger of falling, so I put it at the top of my blouse pocket. The fairy attached to the orchid objects a bit and so I push the orchid further into my pocket, explaining that it will fall out if I don't. Without realizing it, I have begun to make a mistake.

In the evening at the airport, when I find a mailbox inside the terminal, I take the white orchid from my pocket and put it in my Hawaiian guidebook to be mailed home. I have with me a mailing package for the book, and stamps, and I prepare the package quickly and drop it into the mailbox. Now the fairy cries, NO, NO, NO.

Too late. The book is already in the mailbox and I cannot take it out.

NO, NO, NO, cries the fairy again.

What am I to do? I explain that the mail will not be picked up until Monday morning and by that time the flower will be dead. The fairy can leave the flower and go to another flower in Hawaii. It will not be necessary for it to go to the Mainland. The fairy is a bit mollified, but still unhappy, and it is asking where should it go. There are plenty of flowers everywhere, I tell the fairy, even at the airport. A plate glass window is near the mailbox, and on the other side of window is a small, artificially lighted alcove with a couple palm trees. Also some flowers. Go there, I tell the fairy. Go to the flowers in the alcove.

NEVER AGAIN will I take a flower with me. It is too terrible to break their hearts.

———— ◆ ————

A footnote:

A few years later, I am flying on a Korean Airlines plane that should have flown to Asia via Alaska, but a volcanic explosion in Alaska forced the plane to change its route to Honolulu. When we reach Honolulu, we passengers are allowed to briefly stretch our legs in a small, restricted area of the terminal. And yes, guess what restricted area is chosen for us. The place with the mailbox near the plate glass window looking out to the small alcove of palm trees and flowers.

The fairy and its friends are waiting for me! From the small alcove, they are waving and waving to me with great excitement! Such joy for them to see me! Such joy for me to see them!

CHAPTER 6

Tahiti and Rarotonga

Snow is on the ground, the remains of a 14.5 inch storm, as I leave my home on the Mainland to fly to Tahiti, a piece of ancient Lemuria. I ask myself, will today's vibrations of Tahiti have the strong Love energies of former Lemuria? Will the feeling be similar to the island of Kauai? I am optimistic but realistic. I will go to Tahiti with an open mind.

Two places are on my list, the big island of Tahiti Nui that is attached to a smaller island called Tahiti Iti, and the island of Moorea, twelve miles by boat from Tahihi Nui. Of the two places, I think Moorea has a better possibility of retaining pure Lemurian vibrations. I will visit Moorea first.

On my flight to Los Angeles where I will transfer to a direct flight to Tahiti, I sit next to a man of Chinese origin who lives in Singapore, a place I like very much We speak nearly five hours about the culture and politics of Singapore, and by evening, when I board the direct flight to Tahihi, I am ready to sleep the remainder of the way.

We will be landing at Faaa Airport, a few miles from Pepeete, capital of Tahiti, and we passengers are awakened thirty minutes prior to landing. Then, when we are five minutes from landing, the pilot announces we are not ready to land. We circle and circle and circle. I am looking out the window at the dark sky, wondering why we are not landing. Finally the pilot tells us the electrical problem is fixed and we are ready to land. Electrical problem fixed? We have not been told something is wrong with the plane. I am hoping the landing gear has not been our problem. The runway is close to the ocean.

To everyone's relief we land smoothly, and as we disembark, we are greeted by enthusiastic Tahitian singers and dancers dressed in patterned brown and white native dress, floral wreaths on their heads.

It is the middle of the night and I know a boat to the island of Moorea will not leave until morning. Where is the best place to wait out the remainder of the night, I ask, and the answer is simple. Wait just outside the terminal at the outdoor cafe where everyone is waiting. And yes, here are people patiently waiting for dawn, sitting at tables with plastic white chairs, drinking fruit juices and whatever else is offered at this convenient cafe. I learn that at dawn waiting passengers will board Le Trucks, buses that will begin passing the airport to reach Pepeete. From there, boats will go to Moorea.

I sit at a table with New Zealanders waiting to fly to Bora Bora and they watch my bags while I go to a tourist booth for brochures. Here I meet a Rhode Island couple who have just arrived on a Quantas plane from Australia. They say their plane and all other planes were delayed landing until my plane, which their pilot said had undercarriage problems, had safely landed. I think over three hundred people have landed just after we have safely reached the ground. Passport Control was stuffed with Norwegians, French, Germans, and others. Strange to have so many people arriving at the same time in the middle of the night on a Pacific island seemingly close to nowhere.

The Rhode Islanders have been touring Australia and New Zealand, using time/share accommodations, and now they are on their way to Moorea to do the same. When they say they are intending to take a taxi to Pepette port, I tell them the port is undoubtedly closed until dawn. They should join me and the New Zealanders in the cafe to wait for dawn when the Le Trucks begin to run past the airport. This suggestion makes sense to them and they join us.

At the first hint of dawn, roosters begin crowing and I begin to see a hint of red in the sky. Behind the airport, silhouettes of misty, green, exotic mountains start coming out of the darkness, their mysterious presence giving me my first feeling of the vibrations of true Tahiti. A waiting traveler picks up his backpack, walks toward the main road and reaches it just as a Le Truck comes, heading toward Pepeete. It stops for him.

We five, the New Zealanders, Rhode Islanders, and I, pick up our bags, walk to the main road, and as we reach it, a stubby bus comes and stops for us. The driver is a hefty, business-type Tahitian male with an assistant, and the interior of his Le Truck is freshly painted orange with two wooden benches running the length of the interior, each covered by a long cushion. A woman rider already on the bus helps us arrange our bags, and then we are off, headed toward Papeete four kilometers away.

Only three others are on this Le Truck, and no one is waiting to board as we go along. Few stirring at this hour, and when we arrive in the city, it is asleep. The airport is much more active than this place. Blue-uniformed French soldiers are guarding in the airport, but we do not see them on the streets of Papeete. I know there has been recent unrest. Although there is little evidence today, three or so weeks ago, the airport was torched by protesting crowds angry because the French are performing nuclear tests here in Polynesia. Eight have been scheduled since September and three have already occurred. And yes, while I am on Moorea, they explode another, which is a shock to me. I think about the damage to the ocean and its fish. The tremendous noise itself would be awful. Nuclear poisoning would be worse. I wonder if the testers think about this.

Our Le Truck stops in Papeete across the street from a moored Club Med II tourist ship with white sails, and I am thinking this elegant ship probably accommodates 1000. Our driver points the direction to the Moorea ferry quay three or four blocks away, and I begin walking there with the Rhode Island couple. Light rain is falling.

When we reach the ferry quay, we stand under a tarp at the ticket office waiting for the office to open. A number of people are waiting with mounds of luggage. And yes, the ticket woman is coming and she is quickly opening the office and we are buying tickets for passage on a catamaran fast approaching. Actually, there are two approaching catamarans, two-decker, looking exactly alike, belonging to two rival companies. When they dock at a gangplank, I watch as a disorganized array of people, scooters, bikes, luggage are unloaded. Immediately after the last passenger has disembarked, we waiting passengers board, the Rhode Island couple beside me. Our catamaran, new, probably holds 350 people, and because those boarding with us do not reach even a quarter of that number, we sit leisurely on cushioned, airplane-type seats.

At 7:15, our catamaran starts up at full throttle, soon passing a concrete marker to the open sea, and now I am standing at the back of the boat, the roar of the motor deafening, the wind wild from the racing of the engine. The second catamaran roars up behind us and passes us. I watch as Pepeete is fading along with the extensive green shoreline and the tropical mountains above the city. From here, the scenery is exotic.

It is about seventeen kilometers to the island of Moorea, once the home of a powerful chief, and now I am moving to the front of the catamaran to watch Moorea coming into view. I see tall mountains, their vibrations feeling good, and yet, these mountains have a remote feeling. I have not yet connected with them.

When we reach Moorea, both catamarans dock at the same time in a small area soon packed with people, cars, bikes, scooters. I help put the Rhode Islanders, who do not speak French, into a taxi and then I thread my way through confusion to reach the head of a line of four ancient buses waiting to take passengers to hotels and other places. As I board, I ask the driver to tell me when we reach Cook's Bay Resort Hotel, my destination, and he is saying to pull the bus rope when we arrive. In broken French, I explain that he must tell me when we reach my hotel because I do not know the place.

When the ancient bus is loaded with people, we begin our journey, slowly going uphill, the engine grinding, and I am looking out the window at the tropical foliage beside the narrow road. This part of the island is lightly populated. Few cars pass us in either direction. We stop to let off an islander and our next stop is at the Hotel Bali Hai. Soon afterwards, the driver tells me to be ready for the next stop, Cook's Bay Resort Hotel, a colonial-style, two-storied, light green building with lattice on second-floor balconies. This will be my residence for the next couple of days. When I leave the bus, I enter a tropical complex of grass, flowers, trees, tiny fish pools, swimming pool, and a small, yellow, sandy beach. It has everything I would want and more.

I am given Room 144 on the ground floor and my patio looks out at grass and the swimming pool. No time just now to swim. I need to buy food, and I am walking down the road about a half mile, looking at red hibiscus and yellow flowers growing from big green bushes before reaching a grocery store run by an Oriental man from whom I buy beans, yogurt, biscuits, canned fruit salad, and a big bottle of orange drink to give taste to my iodine-treated water.

On my return to the Cook's Bay Resort Hotel, I stop at squashed fruit on the road, its insides a bright orange. This fruit has fallen from a tree with a mighty thump. No birds are eating it. Maybe it is not edible.

I do see large, brown birds with yellow-ringed eyes and yellow beaks, looking somewhat like crows, and later I learn these birds have been brought to French Polynesia to kill wasps, which they do, but they also eat the eggs of other birds. Earlier this morning, from the catamaran, I have seen white, thin-winged, thin-tailed sea birds swooping into the sea. And I have seen flying fish. Tahiti, I know, will have many exotic features, and now that I have my food supply, I am eager to see them.

At the hotel, I go to a footbridge overlooking a shallow pool to watch tiny tropical fish of many colors. I stand and watch them, and at the same time, I am aware of towering mountains in the far background, mist on their tops, heavy tropical foliage on their slopes. The blue waters of Cook's Bay are in my view as well as the expansive Pacific. I am feeling unspoiled vibrations here at this place called Moorea Island, a small piece of ancient Lemuria, and yet, I do not feel integrated with these vibrations. The land is not talking to me. Maybe it will take a bit more time drawing these vibrations into myself before the strangeness goes out of them.

Sunday:

Roosters crow at dawn and, as the light becomes stronger, I look out the window at the towering green mountains, their tops lightly touched with mist. For the most part, the sky is clear. I walk to the small, sandy beach to sit on a reclining chair to watch the ocean and ponder. The water is quiet.

Sunday is church day for islanders. This would be a good time to be with them, to check their vibrations, to see who lives on this island. I have two choices, visiting a Protestant church or visiting a Catholic church. Since the French are predominantly Catholic and were the first Europeans to settle here, I think many islanders follow this religion. I will visit a Catholic church.

When it is nearly church time, I wait in the hotel lobby for a van to pick up guests wanting to attend church. The Protestants will go first. When the van arrives, they climb aboard, the van goes a few feet and stops. Flat tire. It is fixed and then the Protestants are taken to their church while I wait with others to go to the Catholic church called St. Joseph de Pao Pao in the tiny village of Pao Pao. The service has already begun when we finally arrive. The grass in front of the church is jammed with parked cars and pickups and everyone is inside the church singing.

I enter and squeeze into the last wooden pew, an open window behind me, and I am sitting beside a male islander who hands me a white sheet of paper written in both French and Tahitian. It explains the service, which consists mostly of singing. Loud speakers provide background music for the singing. There is no sermon. Communion, yes.

A woman with a heavy cold squeezes in beside me, other members of her family with her. At offering time, a purse is handed through the open window behind me so coins can be dispersed to the family. In the pew ahead of me sits a well-dressed native family, the hefty husband wearing a colorful native shirt. I have noted that many male islanders are hefty. Sitting with him is his wife and daughter whose shiny, black hair is braided, and she wears a starched Sunday-type dress. Another islander has curly black hair and a gold earring in his left ear. He looks like an ex-pirate.

The Polynesians, I have already noted, are loving, family-oriented people. They are modest but not shy. At my hotel are several Tahitian families whose women swim bare-breasted in the swimming pool with their children, their husbands close by. And yes, the Polynesians sing well. This church service I am attending lights up the place with wonderful, strong singing!

The next day:

Mosquito! In the middle of the night, I must put up a net. After that, no mosquito.

I wake before dawn, wait for the roosters to crow, and they oblige. I am thinking they are establishing territory because one crows and the other waits for the finish before starting up.

During the day, the roosters, hens, and tiny chicks scratch for food behind my room. They tend to be quite wild when they feel I am a threat. If I stop to look at them, the hens call their chicks to gather close. I think they have a reason for feeling threatened. Some of them will end up in the soup pot.

Just after sunup, a man laps the swimming pool with steady strokes. It is too early for the Polynesian children to monopolize the pool. They love playing in the water. I walk to the footbridge to see the small fish in the pool below me, and I see elegant, yellow, tiny, angel fish with long delicate fins, and a group of reddish fish hovering at the edge of a rock, ready to dart under the rock when a threat comes. I see fierce, territorial, small, black fish darting at anything coming too close to them. And there are tiny white-breasted, white-snout fish with blue, red, yellow stripes on their backs. An eel, close to two feet long, slides in one coral hole and sticks its head out another.

At 9:30 a.m., I join a tour that circles the island. It would be better for me to circle the island on my own, but no, I will go with others. We drive to a pineapple factory to watch the grinding of fruit, and we are told that on some days only pineapples are ground and on other days only oranges. The juice is put into cartons for sale in stores. We adults are asked to taste pineapple liqueur and the children are given fresh juice. And yes, the fresh juice tastes good! That has been my choice.

Now we are climbing a hill overlooking the Pacific, and we are stopping to take photographs of the ocean with the island of Tahiti Nui in the background. I am looking down at the magnificent light blue sea within a reef that goes far out from Moorea, and then the water beyond the reef turns a dark blue. Our guide says the ocean floor drops 6,000 feet here. This is amazing to me, especially because the mountains here are high, very high.

When it is time for lunch, we stop at a restaurant whose menu is posted at the road. I check the menu prices and they are astronomical, so I decide to sit on a log beside the road to eat my sandwich. Four others join me. Our guide breaks a coconut for us to drink its milk. Tahitian men, he tells us, compete with each other to see who can shuck a coconut the fastest. Some can open a coconut in less than four seconds. When I drink from the coconut he has opened for us, I am surprised that the milk is not particularly sweet.

Across the road are sitting three native women with children. They have taken up residence there to watch the entertainment, us.

When lunch break is over and the tour continues, we stop at Opunohu Bay, which, the guide explains, means the stomach of a stone fish. He says at least one version of Mutiny on the Bounty has been filmed here, and I can understand why. This is a beautiful area. When Captain Cook first arrived, the guide tells us, he sailed into this bay, not Cook's Bay.

Now we are turning off the shore road to enter the interior of Moorea Island, and we are passing an experimental research area being used to find the best trees, plants, animals to thrive on this island. I am happy there is this experimental research area here, and I know Mother Earth would be happy. It is better than experimenting with nuclear weapons.

Magnificent Bali Hai Mountain is in the background when we stop to take photographs of thick-coated sheep. And now our bus is beginning to climb a mountain road, narrow, potted, steep, the bus engine struggling. At the curves, our driver must stop and back up a bit in order to make the turn. We on the bus are quiet, concentrating on the bus struggling up the steep climb through tropical foliage. Our destination is Belvedere Point, and when we arrive, we are greeted by a magnificent view of Cook's Bay to our right and Opunohu Bay to our left, with Mt. Rotui between them. The vibrations are very, very good up here. I am now looking at a chain of pointed, jagged mountains heavy with rain parading diagonally across the landscape. Wonderful to see this!

Our bus begins taking us slowly down the mountain road, and when we are finished with this descent, we are passing pineapple fields where, the guide explains, plants send off shoot-roots, which means the pineapples are producing continually in the fields. We go a bit farther and the guide, as he points out a vanilla vine, says this island was once an important vanilla growing place. It grows like an orchid, he explains, and I am thinking of the old man on the big island of Hawaii who brought so many wonderful plants to his forest garden. He did not show me a vanilla plant, but I think he must have had one. Our Moorean guide tells us that vanilla male and female stamens must touch each other for fertilization, and then a bean is produced. When it is big enough, the bean is dried in the sun for three weeks and it turns black. Three weeks, says the guide, is long enough to make a good vanilla flavor for cooking. A woman on the bus says she has a vanilla plant growing in a basket at her home and she fertilizes it by hand.

The next day:

I wake just before my alarm rings at 4:30 a.m. It is dark. Roosters are beginning to crow. This morning I leave for Papeete, and I want to prepare my departure leisurely. By the time I eat breakfast from my food supply, the sky is light enough to walk to the wooden footbridge to watch the tiny fish swimming in the clear water below me. The red fish are hovering just outside their rock home. The eel is on the move, sliding inside a coral hole and out another. The funny looking, white-snout fish are wearing their red, blue and yellow strips down their backs, and I see a couple yellow angel fish. All is so peaceful.

At 5:50, I am with my bags at the roadside in front of the hotel waiting for public transport to take me to the ferry quay. At 6:15, I am still waiting as a hair-dyed, dark-tanned French women, aged about forty, joins me. She says she is waiting to ride to the ferry with a young man who is meeting someone arriving on the ferry. She says I can go with her.

And so we return to the open hotel lobby to wait and to talk. She is a photographer and producer of films and her large battery-operated sound camera and tripod are being used to film the French Polynesian islands. At 7:15, the young man who will take us to the ferry quay arrives and immediately disappears. When a hotel clerk says he is having breakfast, I look at my watch and wonder if we will be late for the ferry.

A public bus passes the hotel on its way to the quay, and when a second bus passes, I wave to it from the open lobby and run to the road. Fortunately, the driver has seen me and he slowly backs up. The French woman comes with her camera gear and tripod and we both board and are on our way to the quay in this bus, its wooden interior painted a bright orange. An older islander is riding with us, doing a newspaper crossword puzzle, his head wreathed with flowers.

We go slowly along the paved island road, stopping here and there to pick up passengers, and I am looking at the blue ocean to my left. When we reach the quay, a number of people are waiting to board the ferry that has not arrived. I sit on a bench waiting, watching the French woman film fruit vendors before she buys pineapple chunks which she offers to me. Then she buys a papaya with ripe orange insides. She stands and eats this with a big, metal spoon borrowed from a fruit vendor. She says most of her meals are from street vendors.

Two catamarans come nearly simultaneously. When I board the second catamaran, ahead of me is a young Polynesian woman with a white flower behind her right ear. I remember what has been told to me -- a flower behind her left ear means she is looking, and behind both ears means she is married and still looking. What does it mean if she has a flower behind her right ear?

The second catamaran has thirty to forty passengers, and we are soon underway, running full throttle, the other catamaran a bit ahead of us. I am standing at the rear of the boat looking at Moorea Island as we are pulling away. Yes, I am happy I stayed on the island. It is unspoiled and the vibrations are good. I still do not have a close relationship with these vibrations, but maybe this relationship will grow in time.

The sea is a bit rough, unlike the calm sea when I came to Moorea, yet, it is calmer as we approach the Papeete quay. I disembark with the others and I say good-bye to the French photographer now standing in front of a tiny rental car building. Later I see her again and she says there were no rental cars available and so she went to the tourist agency to tell them she is photographing the island and she needs a car and driver. The Ministry of Tourism has immediately supplied her needs.

I cross the Boulevard Pomare (name of the royal family here) to book a room at the Royal Papeete Hotel, and I am given Room 207 overlooking the boulevard and the quay, a good view. From my window, I look at a French military ship, gun metal gray, moored at the quay, and I watch as a French Army truck stops in front of my hotel to pick up eight French military troops wearing khaki. They are staying at my hotel. The truck is painted khaki and at the back is a khaki tarp for protection against frequent showers. I watch as the eight, khaki-dressed troops seat themselves under this tarp. I know that in my hotel lobby a French soldier is on guard. We are well guarded! Tonight I see dark blue military vans cruising the boulevard. The French soldiers stationed in Tahiti have luxury duty, I am thinking, but then I remember the trouble in Paradise here when nuclear testing protesters tried to burn down the airport. For the moment, this problem will not be my concentration. I want to look at this island called Tahiti Nui, where I am staying.

Paradis Tours finds me a tour that circles the island and it begins immediately. I grab my camera and rush downstairs to meet a French and English-speaking Tahitian guide, aged about forty, wearing a bright orange, Tahitian-patterned, cotton shirt. His tour bus is modern, stubby, air-conditioned. We stop at hotels to pick up tour people, and at the Hyatt Regency Hotel, I see this hotel is well guarded by French trucks and troops just inside the entrance to lush grounds of clipped grass and flowering trees. Later, an American couple joining the tour say the hotel is nearly empty. The Japanese, who ordinarily stay here, have canceled, and I assume they are afraid of the trouble.

Our clockwise tour around the island takes us to a tall lighthouse at Venus Point financed by Robert Louis Stevenson's father who wanted to observe there the eclipse of Venus. Hence the name. However, explains our guide, the eclipse was viewed elsewhere. I look at the black sandy coast here being used by a number of sunbathers, who, I think, have come from Papeete because this welcoming beach is close to the city.

As our tour bus circles the island, our Tahitan guides tells us to watch for police cars called 'Sheriff' with one star on them. He says these cars are copying the ones in the former Wild West of the US, and sure enough, we see one on the road near a small police station. I think the idea stems from the movies. At Arahoho we stop to see a blow hole in the slope of a roadside mountain, and we wait expectantly for a roar as steam gushes out of the hole. Sure enough, here comes the roar and the steam. An old woman, a friend of our orange-shirt Tahitian guide, stands nearby selling fruit displayed on a wooden stand. He takes a coconut already punctured for drinking the milk and he is sucking up the milk with a straw as he urges us to buy coconuts from the old woman. She also sells hands of tiny bananas. Expensive! Everything in Tahiti is expensive, I think.

We continue our tour, looking at the blue Pacific to our left and lush green mountains far to our right, and I note with amazement the number of towns and villages we pass. Eighteen in all, says the guide. Too many people for the land, I think. Too many people.

At the Harrison Smith Botanical Gardens, I walk with a British couple and we stop to look at two Galapagos Island turtles. One turtle loves having his throat scratched and stroked, and we oblige his desire. Beautiful gardens here. Red ginger blossoms, lotus flowers in a pond, huge banyan trees, big thickets of tall bamboo, a tropical chestnut tree with nuts on the ground. The Harrison Smith Botanical Gardens is a BIG, well organized place.

At 2:30 p.m. we are in the stubby tour bus going up the coast and I am looking at the white blossoms of the gorgeous roadside frangipani trees. Of all the tropical trees, the frangipani are at the top of my list of favorites. Now we are headed toward the Vaipoiri Grotte, and when we arrive, we stop at two caves, the second having a very, very large mouth and a large water pool. An enchanted place. Gnomes and fairies are living here. Yes, I see them! From an esoteric standpoint, Tahiti has been very quiet since I have been here.

It begins to rain and I take shelter under a tropical tree. Above me are lush green ferns hanging from the roof of the mouth of the cave. Wonderful! Then I run for the bus. I do not have my umbrella and I arrive wet. All of us are wet. Never mind, we will dry quickly in this warm, tropical land.

Now we are approaching an aquarium, and I am walking on a long, curved, wooden ramp over the water, looking down at fish swimming in the shallows of the Pacific Ocean. There are yellow angel fish and tiny blue fish and other fish of many colors. The aquarium itself is actually built under water, the entrance being a plastic shark's mouth, and I am entering this shark's mouth and climbing down stairs to the aquarium to look at fish looking at me.

I see about fifteen sharks, small pink fish, yellow ones, other colored fish, two stone fish, and one big Moray eel. The sharks, when they look at me, seem interested in eating me.

We return to the bus and soon we are passing Faaa Airport as the guide is explaining that faa means big valley. He suggests we look at shop signs along the way because shopkeepers have added an extra 'a' to their signs. An added 'a' means the shop is a big big valley shop. I call this Tahitian humor.

Tahiti is on the verge of escaping me. There is something about the vibrations that do not sit well with me. What is it? Maybe there are too many people with not enough concentration on what is around them -- Nature. My thinking is unfair. I do not know enough about this place. Gauguin liked Tahiti. He has wonderful paintings of Tahiti.

———◆———

The next day:

I wake at 4:30 a.m. to rain pounding on a slanted metal roof just below my window. Later, a series of showers come while I write yesterday's journal. When I finish, I look out the window and see a ferry docking, then passengers walking from the quay. Car traffic begins to increase on Boulevard Pomare passing the hotel and I realize this is morning rush hour. Across the street is a bright red flame tree and beside it is a yellow flowering bush. The boulevard and quay area is beautifully landscaped.

Just after 8 a.m., I am walking to the tourist office to the left of the Moorea quay. A polite young man speaking French gives me a Papeete map and shows me where the municipal market is located and where I can take a Le Truck to the airport. With his instructions firmly in mind, I cross the Boulevard Pomare to the public market, an enclosed building whose ground floor is primarily for selling fruits and vegetables. At one end is a place for selling fish.

At a fruit stall, a shell necklace hanging on a peg catches my eye, and I buy it. When the polite Polynesian girl with no flower behind either ear looks for change, I take a photograph of her stall. Now I go upstairs to look at tourist trinkets, jewelry and wooden statues, and I see that most stalls are not open at this hour. It is too early for tourists. The goods heaped on tables are covered with blue and white printed cloth, and some are covered with red and white cloth. Fortunately, some stalls are open, and I find what I want, a wood-carved Tahitian god, fierce, holding a wooden spear between his legs. Yes, I will take him home with me, and he will sit on my dresser with a god figure from Hawaii, bought at the Kilauea volcano on the big island.

Now it is time to check the Le Truck stop for people going to the airport, and I am walking behind the public market to check for signs of

Le Truck activity. Yes, here is the stop, and yes, here is a FAAA sign in the window of a waiting Le Truck.

I return to my hotel, check out, and walk slowly with my bags, the heat intense now, being careful to avoid puddles, of which there are a number. Already there have been four or five showers this morning. I am walking carefully on the sidewalks, some decorated with concrete swirls reminding me of Portuguese sidewalks, and I am careful to step properly at high curbs. It is amazing how many tourists I have seen walking with canes. One tourist had her arm in a sling. Yes, walking in Papeete is definitely hazardous unless one is careful.

When I reach the back of the public market, I board a waiting Le Truck with a sign FAAA in the window, and this vehicle is empty except the driver, a petite, young Chinese girl with a red flower behind her left ear -- she's available and looking -- and a woman companion beside her with no flower behind either ear. We wait ten minutes for customers, and when we have some, the young Chinese girl begins a slow drive toward the airport, looking for customers. We stop for a young mother to board with her day's old, sleeping child in her arms, her husband behind her. He has a semblance of a mustache and beard, a gold ring on his ear, and his arms and neck are heavy tattooed. I have noted that some Tahitian men wear their hair in a bun.

We are beginning to move a bit faster, and then faster, and we are rattling along the road toward the airport, the young female driver with a flower behind her left ear driving carefully, stopping to pick up and let off passengers. At the airport, when I put the Le Truck money in her hand, she smiles and says 'thank you', then 'good-bye' in English.

I am too early for my flight. Near the Air Tahiti counter a good breeze is sweeping in from the parking lot, and it is here where I wait. I am soon chatting with a young couple, early twenties, he, a blond New Zealander, and she, British. They are on their way to Auckland, having cut short their intended ten-day stay in Tahiti because the place is too expensive for them and they have run out of their budgeted money. The New Zealander says he has been two years in England and now they have started their trip around the world. His dream since childhood has been to come to Tahiti and he has been profoundly disappointed with the place. His dreams are shattered. They do not speak French, they cannot understand what is happening around them or make themselves understood. In Moorea they stayed in a tiny camping spot until they moved to a bungalow hotel where they rented scooters and his girlfriend's scooter shot away with the accelerator stuck. For fifteen minutes they were unable to stop it. When they returned it, they refused to pay and they had a fight with the rental people. Interesting, a tourist told me yesterday she had seen a tourist lying beside the road with a crushed scooter and had summoned an ambulance. Trouble in Paradise! The young couple's problems did not end. They told me they went one night with a tour group to see a Tahitian dance performance, and when it finished, the bus left without them so they had to flag down another bus and insist on being taken to their hotel. Oh dear!

The disappointed couple move along and I am now talking with an American couple from Florida, the woman wearing a flower wreath around her head. She tells me a woman employee at the Moorea Park Royal Hotel where they were staying picked flowers from the hotel garden and then worked one hour to make a wreath for her. It was a gift, the wreath-maker said, and she would not take money. And so, I hear another experience, and this is a good one!

At 4:25 p.m., my plane, three-quarters full, is leaving the tarmac and I take a photograph of Tahiti from the air. Then I make an assessment of the land below me. The vibrations of the island of Tahiti Nui are weakened by too many humans living here and by thousands of tourists coming here. Only the first morning, at the airport, when I watch the dawn come and I see the mist over the mountains, do the vibrations feel good here. The island of Moorea has vibrations that are much better than those at Tahiti Nui, but on the other hand, the Moorean vibrations have their problems, too.

We are flying over the Pacific Ocean, and I am looking at clouds, the long kind, not cumulus, and in less than two hours, we are coming to Rarotonga Island in the Cook Islands. I had not expected our plane to land here, and I am thinking, what a serendipity to be here, even for a short time!

I learn now that this is only a temporary stop for most passengers, but we must all disembark. Wonderful! We take the plane stairs down to the tarmac, pausing to enjoy natives singing and dancing for us, and then we enter the small terminal. Here is a exit we are permitted to use to enter a tiny grass park with flowering trees, and I am entering and looking at this beautiful place. Amid the flowering trees is a frangipani tree with colored flowers. One flower has fallen to the grass, and I am remembering the frangipani white flower given to me during snack time on the airplane. I have it with me in my shoulder bag, and I take it out and lay it on the grass beside its colored frangipani sister. They will be happy together.

I am looking at the mountains of Rarotonga. Mystical, magical! I stand next to a red hibiscus flower, my hands on the park fence preventing me from going further, and I look at the mystical, magical mountains in the distance, the sides heavily forested, tops pointed every which way. Wonderful vibrations coming from these mountains!!! It feels as if no one has ever climbed these mountains, no one has ever disturbed their wonderful vibrations.

Yes, I like Rarotonga very much. I would like to stay and explore this place. But maybe it is best not to see more of this place. Maybe it is best to stand here, next to a huge red hibiscus flower, my hands on the fence, looking at the untouchable, mystical mountains. Maybe getting too close would spoil everything.

CHAPTER 7

Java

I am in Java, Indonesia, to speak with the guardian of Gunung Merapi and the guardian of Gunung Bromo, these two volcanic mountain Beings, in my opinion, important for stability in this area of the Ring of Fire. I prefer these two guardians to be on my side. I am with Margaret and she too will speak with the two guardians.

We have arrived in Jakarta a couple days ago, and this morning we are up at 4 a.m., eating breakfast in our room, and at 5:45 a.m. we are in a taxi taking us to Gambir train station to board a train for Yogyakarta, the closest big city to Gunung Merapi. Our train journey is about an eight-hour ride mostly through rice fields. From our train window, we watch rice being cut by hand, and here and there we see workers slapping the cut plants on a wooden, slatted box so the seeds detach and fall into the box. Other workers are planting by hand straight rows of bright green shoots started from seed, and these new shoots are being planted in fields recently flooded by water. There is so much activity! Some cut fields have drying stubs that turn brown, and these are gathered in piles for burning so the ash can be used for fertilizer. All work is done by hand except occasionally I see a small tractor tilling the land in preparation for plantings. I see no water buffalo until we are close to Yogyakarta.

There are many sick banana trees along the way, and I see many, many, many newly planted papaya and mango trees, which, I assume, will produce fruit substituting for bananas. In Central America there has been success using Agnihotra healing fires to heal sick banana trees. I think this technique is not known in Indonesia.

When we arrive at the train station in Yogyakarta, a big city, we are disembarking just as an older man with a small white beard approaches asking if we need tourist help. Yes. I have learned over years of traveling that the color of this man's hair, white, is a good sign. He will be a stranger to trust, and we follow him to a van with a driver who takes us to a small travel agency store where we book a tour to Gunung Bromo as well as a ride to Bali the day after tomorrow. We make a private arrangement with Sebastian, the white-haired man, to guide us tomorrow to Gunung Merapi.

——— ◆ ———

Next day:

Sebastian and a driver with a van pick us up just before 8 a.m. and we are soon out of Yogyakarta, passing rice paddies, but what soon strikes my eye is steam coming from the towering mountain of Gunung Merapi. It appears to be very active! Its nearby female mate, Merbabu, appears to be inactive.

Our driver stops at a hillside Chinese cemetery with a good view of Gunung Merapi, and I photograph while wondering why there is such a big city, Yogyakarta, so close to such an active volcano. Sebastian says it is only twenty-six kilometers away. I ask if the city ever feels the effects of the volcano and he says a while ago there was such a strong eruption, for three days visibility was so poor, city drivers could hardly see the road.

Gunung Merapi has an active lava dome at its summit and it produces what the natives call Glowing Clouds, more than any other volcano in the world. Glowing Clouds means that the lava dome has collapsed to create an ash flow that goes down the side of the exploding volcano. This ash flow can travel as fast as sixty miles per hour, and it contains highly destructive particles enveloped by gas.

——— ◆ ———

A note:

In addition to volcanic eruptions, there are earthquakes here. A few years after I visit Gunung Merapi, Yogyakarta has a powerful earthquake killing over 4,900 people, injuring 20,000 and leaving 200,000 homeless.

When our van begins climbing Gunung Merapi, clouds hide the mountain and so we can only see tropical forest close to the road. We pass an attractive house whose grounds are well maintained with trees and red flowers, and then we see another expensive, attractive house. I am surprised to find expensive homes on this active mountain. When we pass a large psychiatric hospital with attractive architecture, Sebastian says stress is a reason why many patients are here.

A bit further on, near Kaliurang, we park beside the road and Sebastian begins leading us along a narrow path and over a small bridge to a picnic area and gazebo. Here we can see far below us a big river with little water. He explains that a dam in the process of being built has been badly hurt because of a recent mud slide on the mountain. I am thinking of an ash flow racing sixty miles per hour down the mountain. Later, when we are again in the van and going along, we park it to walk in the forest to Tlogo Muncar Waterfall. Here I see evidence of destruction because of excess water coming over the cliff, which Sebastian tells us is the result of severe storms. Well, at least it is not because of excessive volcanic activity.

We stop at Prambanan to see the ruins of a Hindu temple, and as we are walking on the grounds, we hear loud thundering. We race to our van and jump in just before torrents of rain floods the road. I am amazed how much rain comes so quickly!

By the time we return to our hotel in Yogyakarta, it has stopped. We swim in the pool, shower, and I write in my journal about Gunung Merapi. Tonight, in meditation, I will meet the guardian.

Next day:

7:30 a.m. begins an all-day ride to Gunung Bromo in a van with three others. One is a Dutchman who makes his living guiding Dutch tourists, another is an Austrian who says he has been a hiker ten times in Indonesia and speaks Indonesian, and the third does not speak.

We start our journey SLOWLY, proceeding toward Solo only 65 kilometers from Yogyakarta, but it takes us nearly three hours! Here we pick up a customer who sits in the middle of the front seat, and once he is seated, we FLY, whizzing around everyone. We stay at this harrowing pace all day.

When we come close to Gunung Bromo, the scenery is forested and we are on a mountain road. It is misty, raining, and soon it is dark and we can see nothing. At one point, the rain floods the road, but the flooding stops as we reach a hotel, our destination for the night. It is 7:30 p.m. What a journey!

The hotel is dimly lit inside and out and I do not make a note of the hotel name. This is a mistake. Margaret and I are given a tiny room off an inner courtyard, and we both are so tired, we go to bed immediately. I sleep with my raincoat under me because the sheets are wet.

Early morning:

3 a.m. we wake, dress quickly, and at 3:35 a.m. we board a jeep with two German girls headed toward Gunung Bromo and the coming sunrise. It is raining. There are others in the jeep but it is too dark to see them. At a crossroads, the jeep stops for the two German girls and Margaret and me to leave the jeep to find Gunung Bromo on our own. The driver has another destination for the other passengers and he wants this destination to be ours, too. No. We make arrangements with him to pick us up at the crossroads at 7 a.m. for a return ride to the hotel.

Margaret and I have flashlights, but we soon realize it is too dark for these two lights to be adequate. We begin walking down the steep road ahead of us, but within minutes, we have a dilemma. There is a road to our left going straight up. Should we take that road or should we continue downhill? We consider for a moment and then we opt to go up the hill. We reach a dark house but what do we do now?

In the dark, a man on horseback appears asking if we want to ride horses to Bromo. Yes, Margaret and I will ride horses, but the two German women say no. One of them is afraid of horses. Oh dear! I am hoisted onto a decrepit, old white horse led by a young man holding a rope, and we begin walking, Margaret and the two German women bringing up the rear. We go along in the dark until a man appears holding a rope attached to a horse, and this horse, brown, younger, bigger than my white horse, is for Margaret to ride. As she is hoisted onto its back, Margaret says she has not ridden since childhood. Never mind. That will not be a problem. The men will lead our horses with a rope each. There are no reins for us to use.

We ride only a few moments before the two horses are halted and the men show us how to put one hand behind us to grasp the back of the saddle, the other hand to grasp the front of the saddle. Now the horses begin a sharp descent, and I am holding on tightly. When we reach flat land, we are told to put both hands on the saddle front, and I am doing this as my white horse begins walking on very smooth earth. It is not until we return, when it is full daylight, that I see we are riding across the bottom of a former crater of Bromo that has become flat after it finished exploding.

But now as we are going along in pitch black, we see lights ahead of us, a series of lights. At first I think the mountain is spewing lava, but no, as I come closer, I see the lights are torches carried by men ascending and descending. When I am very close, I see bare-chested Indonesian soldiers carrying torches up and down steep stairs leading to and from the summit of Bromo. An exercise for the soldiers? Strange. A show of protection for tourists? Maybe.

When we reach the stairs, Margaret and I dismount to begin climbing to the summit of Gunung Bromo to witness the sunrise. Our two horsemen assure us they will wait for our return. As we begin ascending, we are passing descending, bare-chested, khaki-panted soldiers carrying torches, some with rifles. We greet each other as we pass, Margaret and I saying 'Good Morning' in English and each replying 'Good Morning' in English. There is something very moving about greeting these torch-carrying soldiers in the dark in what feels like the middle of nowhere.

The sky begins to show its light, and by the time we reach the summit of Bromo, we can see well. We are at a barren summit, standing at a railing looking down at a hole in the crater. Steam is coming from the crater, straight up, not swirling, enveloping us.

It is close to sunrise now. Clouds at the edge of the sky hide the sun but we know it is there. A young man shows us a sunrise offering to Bromo, a small bouquet of orange/yellow marigolds. Yes, we will buy these flowers. Margaret had a dream earlier that indicated she should offer flowers to Bromo, but we have not known how to do this. We have discussed it, but it seemed impossible, under the circumstances of rush, rush, rush and no flowers available Well, thank you, Higher Worlds! Everything has been arranged. The flowers are here at the summit for the sunrise, and yes, we have offered the flowers to Gunung Bromo.

We loiter at the summit reluctant to leave. FINALLY we are here! Much thought has gone into being here at this great home of the guardian named Bromo. Tonight we will meet him in meditation.

When we should not stay another moment, we descend the steep stairs to the waiting horses, and we are once again on their backs, my white horse beginning to follow Margaret on her big brown horse. My old horse tends to fall asleep, and the guide must continually make click-click noises with his mouth to remind my horse that he should stay awake. What my horse needs is a green pasture to spend the remainder of his days!

At the far end of the treeless, flat crater, we climb sharply, I holding tightly onto my saddle, my horse stumbling and stumbling. The men lead us to the Lava View Hotel, and here we say good-bye to them and the horses. At the reception office is a hotel man who understands English, and we are explaining that a jeep has dropped us off at a crossroads in the dark. We have no idea where the crossroads is, but we must find it because the jeep will be picking us up and returning us to our hotel. Does he know where the crossroads is? No.

Well, as an alternative, maybe we can hire transportation to take us back to our hotel. What is the name of your hotel? Oh! We do not know. Where is it? We do not know. We have arrived at the hotel in the rain and the dark and we have left the hotel in the dark to go to Bromo. There were no lights along the way, no distinguishing features in the dark. We do not know anything.

HOWEVER, I have in my pocket the receipt from the Yogyakarta Travel Agency saying Margaret and I are on aYogyakarta-Bromo-Bali trip. I show this receipt to the hotel man, and YES, he knows we are staying at Hotel Bromo. Soon we are in a jeep taking us sharply down the sides of Gunung Bromo, and in about four miles we arrive at Hotel Bromo.

We have breakfast of honey, toast and tea served to us in a barren reception front room, and while we are eating, a rickety mini bus arrives to take us to Bali. Before we leave, the two German women arrive at the hotel and they tell us what happened to them after they witnessed sunrise at Bromo and returned to the crossroads for the jeep pickup. The jeep did not come, and so they tried waving down other jeeps and other vehicles, but no one would stop. They had to return to the Hotel Bromo on foot and they have just arrived. I think Margaret and I have been fortunate! At 9 a.m. we climb aboard the rickety bus and we are on our way to Bali with a full load of passengers.

When it is time for lunch, we stop at a restaurant on a sandy shore. The sea is calm, the vibrations calm, no turbulence whatsoever, and I have time this noon to connect the vibrations of Bromo with those of Merapi -- two, powerful, active volcanoes. Later I see they are 'talking' with each other. Good!!!! When I look at the vibrations of Java, and this includes looking at the aura, which is pastel, predominantly red and blue, the vibrations are not clear or pure but not bad either.

After lunch, our rickety bus is going along the coast toward the ferry port at Ketapang, and we are passing for a long time the forested Baluran National Park whose trees, tall and stately, have been planted by hand. When we arrive at the ferry crossing, it begins to rain. Big rain. In a shelter, we wait with our bags for the ferry to come in and dock, and then we board.

CHAPTER 8

Bali

As the ferry begins its journey, I am standing at the rail looking at this mystical, mountainous, forested place called Bali. The vibrations are compelling, calling to me. Now I am looking at the vast expanse of quiet sea, calling to the dolphins, looking for them, and I do not see them. Margaret rushes to me saying the dolphins are here! They have come to meet us. Where? Here, at the boat, and I am looking down, and yes, they are here. What a wonderful place for them to live offshore from Bali!

This place Bali, yes, it is a mystical place, its vibrations a bit higher than the ordinary third dimensional vibrations of most of this planet. Its residents are closely associated with life in the next dimension, the fourth. Writing these words is too simple. The explanation is much more complex. Yes, very complex, and I am thinking of the vibration called Bali, thinking how creativity holds such an important place here. Thinking how strongly the Balinese people are associated with their mountain guardians, with their gods and goddesses, with their feelings and reverence for Nature. Yes, Bali is a special place, a unique place on this planet. And yes, even though this island is small, because of its unique vibrations, it holds an important position here on Mother Earth.

When we arrive in Bali, it is dark, and we stay overnight in a first available hotel before taking a taxi to our destination, the town of Ubud. In the morning, we drive through Denpasar, capital of Bali, and we are admiring the elaborate, expansive architecture with a strong Hindu influence. I am learning that the primary Balinese religion is an offshoot of the Hindu religion.

For nearly an hour we travel steadily along island roads, and as we approach Ubud, we pass a bird park, a place calling to me to visit before leaving Bali. At Ubud, we take Monkey Forest Road, moving slowly now, looking for the Ubud Inn which my guidebook says is a good place to stay. The road is lined with small tourist shops and many small hotels, and our driver is asking if we want to try one of them. No. Ubud Inn is our destination. The road climbs a bit uphill, and we are proceeding slowly, the three of us are looking for Ubud Inn. YES! Here it is! Our driver parks at a small alcove for cars that has a reception desk and I ask the receptionist if there is room for Margaret and me. Yes. I follow him up a short flight of steps and through an archway that leads directly to a blank wall. We turn 90 degrees to avoid the blank wall and then we go along a pathway through beautiful tropical greens and colorful flowers. At another archway, this one with no blank wall facing it, we turn sharply 90 degrees to walk across a small lawn, passing a tree filled with orchids in full bloom to reach a big bungalow. We walk up steps to a small terrace, and the receptionist opens an elaborately carved teak door to show me where Margaret and I will be staying for the next five days. Perfect!

And yes, there is an outdoor swimming pool at the far end of this complex of bungalows and green lawns and flowering trees, and we are soon swimming in the pool. Paradise!!!

Interesting, we do not discover until our third day that the name of our inn is not Ubud Inn but Ibunda Inn. We three have read the big roadsign in front of the inn and all three of us have read it incorrectly. Amazing! Later, we visit the Ubud Inn and it is definitely not for us. Ibunda Inn is perfect!

After our swim, we cross the road to eat at a family-owned Thai Restaurant. To reach its interior, we climb down narrow steps lined with wonderful tropical foliage and flowers, and then we walk along a stone pathway, passing a small fish pool amid more tropical foliage. Orchids are growing here. We eat in a thatched alcove off the main restaurant seating area, and our waitress is a young Balinese woman wearing a silk brocade sarong, a flower in her hair. We eat fisherman's soup served in heavy native crockery. Crab is in the soup and as I am serving myself, I accidentally drop a small piece of crab shell on the table. Soon a parade of tiny ants are climbing a table leg and crossing the table to reach the speck of soup in the crab shell. Amazing they are so alert! We watch, fascinated, and we do not disturb them. They should have lunch, too. For dessert, we have fried bananas in coconut sauce.

When we finish eating, we walk along Monkey Forest Road to the entrance gate of a big park or animal reserve. This place has many monkeys. We continue without stopping, and then we turn the corner to begin walking uphill, passing tourist shops of woodcarvings, batiks, art, and a musical instrument shop with a sign advertising lessons. We reach a large temple complex behind low walls, and we are standing across the street watching women in Balinese dress climbing stairs to enter the temple complex. On their heads are baskets with floral and fruit offerings. Today is full moon day and I am thinking there will be full moon ceremonies at this temple and at temples throughout Bali.

Next day:

I wake at 7 a.m. to a beautiful morning of bright sunshine and a bit of cool air. It is quiet, peaceful here. As I open the door to look at colorful flowers and bright green tropical foliage, a young man brings fresh floral offerings to the large, standing shrine beside our bungalow. I know this shrine is a spirit house. He is also putting a small offering on the steps to our bungalow before walking to other bungalows to put offerings in the spirit houses and on steps. Another man comes to sweep leaves from the grass and walkway. Everything is tidied up, a morning ritual.

This morning a driver comes to take us in his jeep to the outskirts of the town of Tampaksiring where there are the famous Gunung Kawi shrines carved from rock to commemorate ten Beings. Legend has it that these shrines commemorate members of the royal family. When we reach the site, we climb down a steep stone stairway to the ticket office which is closed. I am remembering there were full moon ceremonies last night throughout most of Bali, and probably ceremonies were held here. Thus, today no one is here.

We continue climbing down the steep stone stairs to reach the Gunung Kwawai shrines, and this is a slow climb with many steps! Shuttered kiosks are along the way, only one open, and no one is there. Now we are passing a small pool with two lotus flowers in full bloom, and finally we reach Gunung Kawi. We are looking at these ancient Hindu-style, rock carvings here at a river embankment as well as another set across the river.

We are coming to an open kiosk and stopping to look at hangings of wonderful, hairy masks. The owner is squatting outside the kiosk, working on a curved, ceremonial bamboo pole about fifteen feet long with something dangling at the end. Later, along the roadway to the town of Batur, we see many of these curved poles with something dangling at the end.

At the ruins of an ancient temple complex, we take off our shoes to enter. The damp, green moss growing on the stones feels good to our feet, and yes, it feels good to be at this ancient place, and even better because we are alone. Our guide will not enter this temple. He says he only enters 'his' temple, meaning, the temple he is associated with. Colorful red and dark blue roosters are perched on the wall of this ancient place. I remember there is much cock fighting in Bali.

Afterwards, our driver takes us to the Tirta Empul temple complex, an extensive complex, and here, to our surprise, we realize we are at a sacred spring whose source is an active volcano. The spring is bubbling and bubbling as we watch, and, within a few feet of each other, we see three boiling, mud pots. Margaret sees a nearly five-foot white eel, a Balinese sign of good luck. Tiny fish are swimming here and there, and at one place is bright green grass with lotus blossoms. I am amazed to see the grass and lotus here because the water contains much sulfur. Our driver tells us the Balinese believe the spring has special powers and people come here to be healed.

Now our driver is putting us in his taxi and driving us to the town of Batur. When we arrive, it feels as if the entire town is walking to a temple on the Gunung Batur volcano to hold ceremony at the time of the full moon. Yes, I think close to 1000 are dressed in colorful Balinese clothes, baskets of offerings on their heads. Police are keeping order and our driver tells us to roll up our windows and to not take photographs.

Gunung Batur is the second most important volcano in Bali, and I can understand why the people are honoring it, because, when it erupts, it erupts hard. In 1917 its explosion killed thousands of people and wiped out 60,000 homes and 2000 temples before it stopped at the entrance to the village temple, according to my guidebook. When it erupted again, it covered the newly built village.

Later, when we near the town of Kintamani, we stop at a roadside lookout that gives us a panoramic view of Gunung Batur with a big scar of brown/black lava on its slope. I see a small vent of steam coming from this volcano.

Tonight, in meditation, I speak with the guardian of Gunung Batur.

Next day:

This place, Bali, is in tune with all aspects of Nature. The Balinese are not blind to the unseen worlds; everything is respected. Offerings are made to keep away evil spirits, and these offerings are placed in many, many places. They offer incense, flowers, and sometimes yellow rice. Our white-tiled, terrace floor as well as steps leading to the terrace have yellow rice offerings. Flower offerings are in the middle of the archway before we reach our bungalow, on the steps near the swimming pool, on sidewalks, in front of stores and buildings and spirit shrines. Daily, new offerings replace earlier offerings.

This noon our driver takes us to the Taman Burung Bali Bird Park, home of birds of over 250 species. Some, such as red parrots, white parrots, and macaws, sit on the arms and shoulders of park attendants for the benefit of tourists. These are friendly, obliging attendants, and the perched birds seem happy to be with them. I see here at the park twenty red ibis, some white ibis, eight South African sarus cranes, two red pheasants, bright yellow birds, bright blue birds, and many other birds of various colors and sizes. Yes, this is an astonishing place! The birds seem well cared for, well housed. What a pleasure it is to see all these beautiful birds!

Next day:

Tremendous rain all night. Probably an inch an hour, and I am thinking Mother Earth is cleansing herself here in Bali. When I open the teak doors to look out this morning, I see our front yard of grass is flooded and the sidewalk is flooded here and there, much to the disgust of a semi-wild cat who has to change his usual walk pattern. A huge spider who has spun his huge web trap in foliage about twenty feet from our bungalow is waiting for his meal, the web having survived the rain without damage. Birds are flying here and there, some darting very close to the spider's web, but I think they know about this trap because they do not become victims.

Margaret and I sit on our terrace looking at this wonderful scenery while we discuss today's meditation, the energizing of Bali as a new world archetype that has perfect balance between Nature and Man. A new pattern for Mother Earth, a new thought form, a sunrise, a new beginning. We speak of volcanoes, Mother Earth's way of making NEW EARTH (New world). The fire/volcanoes are a way for her minerals and her fertility to be sent as ash/fertilizer across the land so the plants can receive strong nourishment, so the people and animals who eat these plants will be strong.

LOVE for the earth is here at Bali, a necessary ingredient to form a perfect balance between Mother Earth and humanity. This balance encourages strong vibrations that can be used to form a perfect archetype for a new world pattern/thought form.

I stop short at putting these new vibrations over the current vibrations of our 'old' world because the head guardian at Gunung Agung, the largest, most important mountain here in Bali, has not been properly visited or consulted. Tomorrow we will visit Pura Besakih Temple on the slopes of Gunung Agung.

Now I am meditating on Gunung Agung, called Mother Mountain, navel (the place of birth) of the world, and I am opening to the male guardian, calling him Agung. He an older man, strong, imposing, not humorous, and I am telling him the position of the planets next month (May 2000) will cause stress for Mother Earth. He answers gruffly that the stress is already felt, and I am saying there is a need for cooperation among all volcanoes at the Ring of Fire in order to temper coming activity. He answers that he does not know any others except in Bali.

I am feeling the presence of the other guardians of volcanoes on this island, especially the ones at Batur and across the land at Danau Bratan, and I am thinking that if they do not know guardians outside Bali, what is there to do?

I ask Agung if he knows Pele, and yes, he knows her. She will be the conductor, I tell him, the orchestra leader of the Pacific Ring of Fire guardians. Would he, Agung, follow under her baton? He agrees.

And so, there is a solution.

---

9 a.m., we are in the driver's jeep, heading toward Gunung Agung and the relatively new temple on its slopes. In 1963, an eruption destroyed the temple except two small statues, ancient animal guardians, standing side by side. I am thinking about these two guardian statues as our driver is threading his way through slow truck traffic and chaotic motorcycle traffic. We see people dressed in their best Balinese-style clothes, offerings on their heads, walking to the temples.

We are driving through Gianyar, then going to Semarapura where Indonesian flags fly above city streets and there are some big monuments. I think probably this is a government city. Now we are turning north and climbing, climbing, climbing a twisting, mountain road. When we reach a lookout, we stop to take photographs of the sea in the far background before continuing, upward, always upward. Now we enter a town where elegantly dressed people have offerings on their heads. This is a funeral procession. The casket is covered.

When we pass Pasaban, we see Gunung Agung straight ahead, a cloud nearly covering its top, and when we arrive at Besakih to climb to the temple complex called Pura Besakih perched on Agung's slopes, the mountain top is completely covered with clouds.

Our driver parks the jeep and Margaret and I begin dressing in ceremonial clothes. I put on a blue sarong bought a couple days ago, and Margaret puts on her red and yellow sarong. Our driver helps us, his skilled Balinese hands knowing exactly how to we should be wrapped in these unfamiliar sarongs. When he is satisfied we are dressed properly, we leave him to begin walking to the temple. A man approaches asking to guide us and we accept. We should have a guide, our driver has told us, because that is how the people make money. This island, he has explained, gives few chances for many to make money.

Our guide is a young man with bleached, blond hair and we are walking with him about one half kilometer, always ascending, before entering the temple complex itself. He explains there are temple sections. Here, where we are standing, is the section commemorating Brahma, controller of fire/red, and then there is the section commemorating Shiva, controller of white/yellow/destroyer/wind, and then begins the Vishnu complex, black/water.

Of particular importance to us is a black, stepped, pagoda-style temple, its shape signifying the mountain, and here are the remains of the two small animal statues that were not destroyed in the 1963 eruption. We are told that forecasters predicted the eruption of Gunung Agung, but it was disregarded because Soeharto, then President of Indonesia, was more interested in impressing foreign travel agents with the treasures of Bali, including Pura Besakih, which was ready to have an important celebration. And yes, the celebration was held, foreign travel agents came, and Soeharto came with great fanfare. When the celebration was over and everyone left, Gunung Agung erupted.

We ask if we can meditate at the only remaining relics of that explosion, and yes, we are given permission. We enter a tiny enclosure to sit in front of the two tiny statues draped in black and white checkered cloth, and a priest dressed in white, a white cloth on his head, comes to officiate. We sit cross-legged behind him as two identical offerings are placed in front of us -- a white flower and a red flower and a green sprig -- one offering for Margaret and one for me.

Our guide gives us instructions. First we must place the red flower in our hands and raise our hands in Balinese prayer style. The priest, his back to us, says some words. Then we must offer the white frangipani flower in Balinese prayer style, and then the green sprig. Now we are told to put the flowers behind our ears and we have done this. Rice is put on our foreheads to signal that we have performed the proper ceremony here at Pura Besakih. We meditate a few moments longer and I am speaking to Agung.

Today is the 20th day of 21 of a ten-year ceremony here and the ceremony is called Betar Turum Kebah. How fortuitous we are here today!

We have arrived in Bali at the full moon of the tenth month of the Hindu calendar, a time of great ceremonies during this auspicious moment. Today, here on the slopes of Gunung Agung, it is no exception. Many, many people are here, dressed in gorgeous, new, colorful sarongs, carrying offerings on their heads.

Beautiful day! No rain today. I think Mother Earth feels herself clean enough here.

We leave the temple complex and walk downhill to our jeep, say good-bye to our guide, take off our sarongs, and we are ready to thread our way back to Ubud in slow traffic.

2 p.m. lunch at the Thai Restaurant. Glass noodles, dish of tiny shrimp, garlic cashews in soy sauce, large bottle of mineral water, fried bananas with coconut sauce, plate of exotic mixed tropical fruit. The restaurant people have been very kind to us these past few days. They shake hands with us when we leave, knowing we are leaving Bali, and they are asking us to return.

We do not see the humming bird today and this is the first day we have not seen it. I have been teasing Margaret because the first time we came to the restaurant, she swished it from our table, thinking it was a bee. Since that first poor start, the busy humming bird has been with us every noon except today. Maybe he is sad we are leaving.

We stop at a pharmacy close to the Ibunda Inn to buy balsam salve to ease the itching of a large bite on my thigh. Heat has made it worse and now it is huge. The pharmacist takes a quick look, says it isn't serious, and recommends balsam salve. I have been asking for Tiger Balm, which was successful earlier in China, but the Balinese pharmacist has none. He says balsam salve is similar and he asks me to smell it. Yes, I need no more convincing. I buy it and it is successful.

6 p.m., we are sitting on our bungalow terrace knowing the sun is ready to depart. Some clouds, a hint of a cool breeze. A mourning dove is cooing nearby, cicadas are sounding, and a semi-wild cat is walking by. These cats are interesting. They are scrawny and I assume they have worms because of the roughness of their very short hair. These cats are small, of different colors, always foraging for food and seemingly to belong to no one. The one distinguishing mark of all cats that parade down the walkway

in front of our bungalow is that they have one half to three quarter length tails.

Landscapers squatting to do their work have just used short hand scythes to clip our lawn grass. They are now beginning to snip at dead branches on nearby trees, but they do not touch the palm tree in the center of our tiny lawn. I look at the small, purple, orchid blossoms, six to a stem, growing on the palm tree. Beautiful, beautiful, beautiful here in my Paradise. And yes, I must mention the green plants resembling elephant ears with bright red veins lining the front of our white-tiled terrace.

Fresh offerings of flowers, different ones from this morning, are on the terrace, just above the last step, three feet from where I am sitting, writing my journal. Dusk is coming fast now. Tomorrow we leave Bali.

CHAPTER 9

Japan -- Oshima. Sakurajima. Mount Fuji

OSHIMA ISLAND:

A few years ago, when major tectonic plates in the Pacific Ocean located west of Tokyo showed excessive energy, I phoned Kathleen to help release it. Soon afterwards I went to this area, specifically to the island of Oshima, to form an alliance with the main goddess there, to ask her help in maintaining a balance of energy in her region of the Ring of Fire.

------◆------

Here is my Oshima Report:

Today is a foggy, dull day, which I understand is typical of the rainy season in Japan. At the Tokyo port I am boarding a rainbow-painted ferry to take me to the island of Oshima. I am sitting on the lower deck looking at big cranes, big cargo ships. Everything is orderly, as would be expected at a Japanese port. When the rainbow-painted ferry reaches open water, I am happy the Pacific is calm today, and I am looking out at the waves on this dull day. As we approach Oshima, the sun is trying to poke its way out of the clouds, and when we reach land, it greets us.

I am looking at this place called Oshima, taking in the vibrations, and I am thinking I am witnessing a piece of ancient Lemuria. Tropical foliage is delicious to the sight. The flowers are gorgeous and many are unique to my eyes.

I am being driven to an islander's house on an unmarked, rutted, muddy track in uncut tropical foliage. When I reach the place, I take off my shoes and step into a room with a low table, cushions around it. A floor TV is showing a movie of ceremonies honoring the goddess of the island's volcano. Males dressed in special regalia are respectfully honoring her, and at one point a male child dressed as a girl is the center of attention. Women wearing colorful native regalia perform a female ceremony. I watch this as I sit with others on floor cushions around the low table, drinking green tea, eating from bowls of fruit. Two lively cats play nearby.

It begins to rain. Tropical rain, heavy, warm. We speak of the rain purifying the island and especially the volcano, Mount Mihara, an active volcano that last erupted a few years ago. My need is to go to the summit not only to ask the goddess of this volcano to help keep steady the tectonic plates within her jurisdiction, but also I need to ask her to keep the volcano quiet.

I know Oshima is too dry, a condition similar to when the volcano last erupted. I am happy it is raining. Through the window, I watch the plants absorbing this great necessity of life. The goddess and her plants will be offered water at the summit of the volcanic mountain.

When it is time to give offerings, we gather water at a sacred spring at the base of the island, and we take this to the summit. In the rain, a van drives us up the mountain road, and we are winding round and round the slopes, looking at heavy green foliage and bright, colorful flowers. When we reach a summit lookout, in ceremony we offer the sacred water to the goddess as we pour it on the plants of the land. She is HAPPY to see us! We are feeling her LOVE, that great Lemurian gift!

In meditation, by using the vibration of olive oil to lubricate, we help to oil Mother Earth's creaking joints, her tectonic plates. Man has been misapplying Mother Earth's oil resources for power and selfish reasons. All causes have effects. Yes, we have lubricated Mother Earth's creaking joints.

A Japanese woman who lives here on Oshima is using delicate gongs to clean the vibration here. Native American SilverStar standing beside me is using her rattle to take negative vibrations off the aura of the goddess, and now I am sounding the Aums strongly, using a slightly higher tone than usual, concentrating on 4th dimensional energies, home of her aura. The others are joining me. Seven times we sound the Aums, concentrating on the aura. POWERFUL what we are doing. I am hearing the resounding in the 4th dimension. The third through the fifth dimensions are affected. YES. The goddess is happy! When we are finished, we are HAPPY. This work is satisfying.

Within a week, the vibrations of the goddess here at Oshima will be joined with the god/male vibrations at Sakurajima, the most active volcano in Japan. That is another piece of the journey to tell later.

When we leave the Mount Mihara summit, we drive down the mountain to a small museum to see an extensive exhibit of camellia flowers. I walk from display to display looking at SO MANY different types of camellias. Wonderful!

———◆———

Next day:

Today is beautiful, sunny, hot, a good day to visit a seaside cave. I am told an old man used to live in the cave. Some islanders claim to still see him even though he died many years ago. To reach the cave, we drive on mountain slopes adorned with gorgeous hydrangeas planted along the tropical route. Then, for some unknown reason, about an eighth of a mile before the cave, the road is closed to traffic and we must proceed on foot.

A large troop of monkeys cross the road in front of us just as we begin to walk slowly downhill. They do not stop. As we proceed, we are looking at the lush, tropical, green land. In one place, a wide strip of black sand covers the green plant life and I realize that molten lava has come here from an earlier volcanic eruption.

We stop to admire a great bunch of large flowers growing on one bush. I do not recognize them. I am thinking of this land we are on, this island called Oshima, so remote, living by itself in the Pacific, a piece of Lemuria, and I am thinking these flowers ARE a preserved piece of pristine, ancient Lemuria. Yes, the vibration of Lemuria is very strong here. Pure, pure, pure. It is as if I have climbed back in time, climbed back into ancient time.

We photograph the gorgeous flowers, so many clustered on one huge bush, mainly blue in color with individual clusters of tiny white flowers on the blue flowers. I am thinking of the brilliance of creativity that has made such remarkable flowers.

Now we are at sea level, and we are climbing steep concrete stairs to reach a walkway built into a stone mountain cliff. This walkway gives us access to the cave resembling a wide open mouth. It feels sacred, like a huge altar, and yes, at the back of this mountain cave, I see a manmade altar with offerings.

I am walking up wet steps to enter the cave and just inside the cave I reach a bit of water, like a miniature pond, with tiny green pods growing on the surface of the water. I know these are ancient plants, speaking plants, healing plants, and my stomach welcomes them. It is a bit bothered by trying to digest unfamiliar Japanese food, such as rice rolls with bright blue/purple something, probably ground beans. I am bringing the energies/vibrations of these tiny green, Lemurian pods into my stomach, and instantly -- SWISH. These tiny green pods filter from my stomach everything that is unwelcome. AMAZING. Thank you!

When I am leave the cave, I sit on a tall rock outside this ancient Lemurian place. So powerful are the Lemurian vibrations! And now I am opening to the headquarters of the Nature Spirits, the fairies, in the rain forest of Malaysia, at the waterfall. I am connecting the Oshima Nature Spirits with this headquarters, these Oshima Nature Spirits having forgotten their connection with the headquarters, and I am linking them, joining them. They will no longer work alone. They are part of a vast network of Nature Spirits, fairies, all being reconnected to the headquarters.

It is time to leave the sacred cave area, and I am returning to the walkway cut into the side of the stone mountain cliff, climbing down the steep concrete steps, walking on the stony shore, the ocean steps away. I begin hearing the talking stones, small black stones in the water at the shore. When the waves come in strongly, these small black stones are pushed inland, and when the waves retreat, the small black stones make a talking sound as they roll back into the water. I watch the coming and going of the small black stones. I listen to their talking sound. I am fascinated! They remind me of the talking mountains at Rio de Janeiro.

Here at Oshima, this island, this place of purity, the vibrations are good. A piece of ancient Lemuria. My heart feels this.

I begin walking up the somewhat steep road until I come to a circular gate that opens to an outdoor zoo where animals roam free. I hear monkeys making a big noise. I cannot see them but I can hear them. When I turn the circular gate and enter the zoo, the monkeys become silent.

I can reach the van by walking through the zoo, but I hesitate. I remember the monkeys at the top of Gibraltar. I have climbed up to give peanuts to them, and yes, they have come for the peanuts, but instead of wanting single peanuts each, they wanted the entire bag immediately.

They grabbed it and scampered away. One monkey tried to take my purse.

Yes, here at Oshima, at this outdoor zoo, I have second thoughts about walking through the zoo. I turn the circular gate to leave and then I continue along the road to the van. Not a sound comes from the monkeys. I know they are telepathic and they can read my thoughts that I do not trust them.

I am sad as I walk along the road. Maybe they are sad, too. My birth year puts me in the Chinese year of the monkey. For them, perhaps they think I am a human monkey. I have said no to them, and they are silent. Yes, I know they have telepathically read my thoughts.

4:45 p.m. this afternoon, I board the rainbow-painted ferry to return to Tokyo.

SAKURAJIMA:

I am at the Hiroshima Train Station in the early morning ready to journey to the southern tip of Kyushu Island to talk with the guardian of Sakurajima, the most active volcano in Japan. This volcano is part of the Ring of Fire and so it needs to be contacted for the benefit of all who live at the Ring of Fire, for the benefit of Mother Earth, and for all humanity.

We live during dangerous times. Mother Earth must contend with serious misdeeds of humanity. A misuse of Mother Earth's resources is a violation of the laws of Nature. Since all have a consciousness, including Mother Earth, one can expect a reaction when Mother Earth receives a stomachache from misuse of her resources. Humanity can expect volcanic eruptions, earthquakes, tsunamis, and weather-related events such as typhoons and drought.

I am recalling an incident that happened several years ago in South America. The weather was in an uproar when suddenly a sea of mud began racing down a mountainside swallowing everything in its path. This happened so quickly, there was no time to prepare.

A fire healing center was in its path, but when the sea of mud reached the center's parking lot fence, it abruptly swerved to avoid the parking lot, even the fence, and then it continued on its way down the mountain. Agnihotra fires, healing fires, had been burning there regularly at sunrise and sunset for many years. Was the avoiding of the healing center by the sea of mud a coincidence? I think this was no coincidence. It is an example of Mother Earth taking care of her children. When they behave in a kind and gentle manner, with respect for the land, with respect for her, she will take care of her children.

And so I am heading this morning to Sakurajima, the most active volcano in Japan, to speak with the guardian of this volcano, to point out the need for discretion in the days to come. I am traveling with my friend Margaret, and because we speak or read no Japanese, we make our share of train-ride mistakes this morning before we reach the ferry terminal that will take us to Sakurajima, located on a small island.

At the ferry terminal, we watch as a big ferry comes for us, and then we board with a half dozen other passengers. We choose to sit at a round table on the deck facing the big volcano of Sakurajima looming a few miles ahead of us. A young man in his late twenties comes to the table and asks in English if he can sit with us. Yes, of course. We are delighted to have someone sit here who speaks English, and we are soon learning that he is a poet who has spent time in Los Angeles as a caretaker for an elderly Japanese couple. He says he enjoyed taking care of them. I ask why he is going to Sakurajima and without hesitation he says he is going to Sakurajima to speak with the guardian.

I am surprised, and I am saying I have also come to speak with the guardian. I tell him our guidebook says there is a Visitor's Center near the pier and our intention is to go to this center to look at displays of the volcano in order to know the volcano. Does he want to come to the center with us? Yes.

The ferry crosses the water and within fifteen minutes it reaches the shore and docks. The young man asks in Japanese how to reach the Visitor's

Center, and he is given instructions which we follow as we are walk along the island's roads noticing such lack of pedestrian needs as sidewalks. We enter a modern, nondescript building that is actually a small museum, and here we sign the Visitor's Book before entering a small, circular room, alcove, to watch a dramatic film of the volcano beginning to growl. Then it growls loudly, and then it explodes LOUDLY. A tremendous explosion, force, of fire! Amazing to see this true-to-life view of how the volcano explodes. I watch this drama a half dozen times, absorbing it.

Our English-speaking companion has departed and Margaret and I spend time looking at the artifacts before leaving the museum to walk on a pathway paralleling the shore. We see great rocks thrown here by the explosion of the volcano towering above us to our right. I am looking at this great Sakurajima volcano, and I am connecting to the male guardian of this place. He is friendly. And yes, later I will join him with the goddess of Oshima. For a balance, for a balance of energies.

We come to a covered pavilion with four wooden tables, three in use by Japanese visitors and the fourth has a small black bundle, indicating that we should not sit there. I sit on a concrete ledge at the end of the pavilion and Margaret sits outside the pavilion. We are both facing the volcano, which, actually, as I am examining it, consists of three volcanoes.

I am thinking on this place, making friends with this guardian of the most active volcano in Japan, this volcano sitting on the Ring of Fire, and I am remembering a couple months earlier when I worked with Sakurajima to steady it when there was danger to the North. Now I am here.

I am surprised as our English-speaking friend walks to the pavilion from the shore. I have not seen him at the shore. We have not passed him. He comes to the fourth table to claim his black bundle and then he seats himself barefoot on the floor of the pavilion, opens his bundle, and takes out a pack of bright white rice paper, ink and a brush. He tells me he is ready to make a poem written in ancient calligraphy for the guardian of Sakurajima.

I watch him take from his bundle a long, thin, black scarf and wind it around his head so it fits tightly to his skull, the long ends going down his back, and then he seats himself in a cross-legged position and immediately enters a trance. He begins rapidly writing his poem in ancient calligraphy on the bright white rice paper. Amazing!

When he finishes, he asks me to sit in front of him so he can write a poem for me, and I am obliging, seating myself with my back to him, looking at the volcano. But no, he wants me to face him, my back to the volcano, and so I oblige. He points to his third eye to show me where I should look at him. Yes, I understand. Now I am going into meditation as he is going into a trance to rapidly write a poem in ancient calligraphy on the bright white rice paper. It takes no more than two minutes for his poem to cover the rice paper.

When he finishes, he comes out of his trance and begins reading to me the ancient calligraphy message: 'Bright Light lady, emit your love to the universe and save the people of this planet. Save the minds of the people of this planet with your Light.'

Now it is Margaret's turn to sit before the poet, and she obliges as he rapidly writes a poem for her in ancient calligraphy. It is translated into: 'Your pain becomes joy! With your love and compassion, hug the pain of many people with your love and compassion. It is your wonderful work.'

We thank this remarkable man, who is, I realize, a personification of the guardian of the volcano itself. A very, very ancient person here. Very, very ancient. Before we leave him, he draws with his brush the number 100,000 on rice paper, and he tells us that this is the number of people he is intending to meet to write poems. He says, when he reaches his goal, there will be peace. Yes, a remarkable person has been sent to us today!

Just as Margaret and I are ready to leave the island of Sakuajima to take the fifteen-minute ferry ride back to the mainland, Margaret sees smoke puffing from the volcano. Hello, we call to Sakauajima! I am making a joke that the guardian is smoking a cigarette. We watch as the smoke turns into a cloud with the shape of a heart. Yes, it is a beautiful gift for us. Great Love is coming from the volcano! Thank you!

Later, I join Sakurajima to Mihara of Oshima.

MOUNT FUJI:

The Solstice:

Last night I sleep with twenty others on floor pallets in a modern, wooden house near the foot of Mount Fuji. We are here to observe today's Solstice activities. Before 9 this morning, everyone has left the house except me and three Japanese maintenance women who, before leaving, bring me a plate of fruit.

Outside, a typhoon rages, the wind sharp, the rain heavy. It has been raging for hours. The temperature on this first day of summer is warm, comfortable.

With my ear phones, I listen to soft music as I begin to program the vibrations of peace and love to Fuji Typhoon, as I call this fierce storm raging outside. With my mind, I program peace and love to every droplet of rain, and I am visualizing Fuji Typhoon moving across the land putting down these vibrations of peace and love.

This big typhoon is not an angry typhoon. And yes, one can talk to this typhoon, but I do not. Instead, I program peace and love and I am visualizing this peace and love saturating the land and saturating the nearby Pacific Ocean. I am visualizing the wind helping to carry the programmed peace and love droplets of water across the land and to the sea and then across the entire world.

The door opens and the three maintenance women enter. The one who speaks some English says they will be in the house only a couple minutes and then they will leave and not return. Interesting that this should happen just now as I am programming the water droplets with peace and love. Over 80 percent of the human body consists of water, and I am thinking there is no coincidence that these three women have appeared just now. They represent the human race and they are receiving the peace and love vibrations being sent out just now. In effect, they are taking these vibrations to the entire human race because All are One.

A note: About ten years ago, I was attending a Native American conference in Janesville, Wisconsin, when we received a phone call warning that a hurricane was ready to strike Galveston, Texas. It needed to be turned away. Will we help? Of course.

Immediately we went into meditation, each in his own way to stop what was ready to happen. We stayed in meditation about a half hour and then we returned to conference matters. Later, we received another phone call. The hurricane had swerved away from the city. Galveston was spared.

It is true that as far as I know, here, in Japan where I am, no one has asked Fuji Typhoon to dissolve or go away. It was accepted, for whatever reason. Maybe to cleanse the land. Interesting, the next morning, all is still. Sunshine reigns. When we look out the window to admire the sunshine, we see Mount Fuji, wearing a double cap of brilliant white clouds. The saying is that when these clouds descend the mountain to make a ring around the mountain, this is a special moment. A shaman of the Ainu indigenous tribe of Japan is with us and she tells us that when the clouds descend to make a special ring around the mountain, gold will come from her hands for healing the people. Sure enough, I see this gold appear on her hands.

CHAPTER 10

New Zealand

I am flying to Auckland, New Zealand with Margaret, and as the plane is ready to land, the sun is taking a holiday and the sky is dull. I look curiously down at this land, thinking about the last time I flew here, during Commonwealth games. Excitement was in the air. Queen Elizabeth was attending them as well as visiting a horse farm. This morning begins an ordinary day as our plane wheels touch the tarmac at 11:30 a.m.

Passport control is quick, but we wait with our bags for a time in the 'Anything to Declare' line while vigilant customs people scan mounds of luggage being brought into New Zealand by Samoans. When it is our turn to say what is in our bags, we declare granola and peanut butter. I worry about declaring food. Customs is not interested.

A mob of people are in the terminal waiting for friends and family. We change money and then we check with Hertz for a rental car. Yes, here is a car for us, blue, and we are putting our bags in the trunk. I will drive because Margaret has never driven on the wrong side of the road, as I call it, and so it is best that she doesn't start learning on this journey. Before we start, we need to figure out how to make the lights work, where are the direction signals, windshield wiper lever, air conditioning, radio, etc.

Okay, time to bite the bullet, and I am starting the car, and moving it slowly from its parking place just as another car is leaving the parking area. I follow him, telling Margaret I do not know exactly which side of the road I should be on except I know she should be riding in the ditch. If she is riding in the ditch, we are okay. This is an old teaching from my mother who taught me how to drive in the Cayman Islands, but there was one big difference in the Caymans. There, I drove a USA car with the steering wheel on the left. Now, in New Zealand, the steering wheel is on the right, and so the passenger, rather than the driver, needs to be riding in the ditch. Margaret is a little slow understanding that riding in the ditch is humor, yet the concept is important.

Well, here we go! Happy landings for both of us!

Margaret has maps in her hands to guide us to Route 20 as we leave Auckland Airport, but where are signs for Route 20? There are signs for Hamilton, but none for Route 20. And, here comes a 'round about'. Which road takes us to Hamilton? Does the Transport Department think we all live in New Zealand? We are going along anxiously. Ah, here is a sign to Route 20. And a sign for the Expressway. Good. I am driving on the Expressway, joining the traffic, all going fast, and I am going fast with them, reading signs for turnoffs, these signs too close to the turnoffs so we are caught on wrong lanes. Stress! Here is a mileage sign for Hamilton, 109 kilometers, farther than I had thought. Finally we reach Hamilton and we are beginning to follow signs to the Waitomo Cave, our destination. Now we are coming to Otorohanga, a difficult name to pronounce, and soon afterward we reach Waitomo.

Our first objective is to buy tickets for the 5 p.m. last tour of the day to the Waitomo Cave that will show us the Glowworm Grotto. Because we are early, after buying our tickets, we seat ourselves on a wooden bench at the base of a huge, old red bark tree, reminding me of a Redwood, and we are looking around at mystical green tropical foliage. Some ferns are as tall as trees. A small river is below us.

When the tour begins, fifteen of us, mostly New Zealanders, are guided by a dark-haired, early twenty's Maori who takes us into the dark cave lighted by electric lights. We stand in awe as he explains the limestone stalagmites and stalactites, and we are looking at an area called the Cathedral cavern with its long-stemmed, white, hanging stalactites. The guide tells us opera diva Kiri Te Kanawa once sang here.

I love caves. I love to feel the coolness of them. I love to see the beauty of them.

We are walking to the spectacular Glowworm Grotto as our Maori guide patiently explains about the glowworms and what we will see. In the dark interior where there is water, we climb aboard a boat, and he silently glides us along the dark water. We are silent, too, so as not to disturb the glowworms. The ceiling here is low, just above our heads, and we are gliding along looking in awe at the tiny glow over our heads, like a vast network of lights, a miniature sky of stars on the darkest of dark nights. Fantastic sight to see these glowworms!

Tomorrow afternoon when we visit the museum here, we will learn that this cave was once under water, part of the ocean, and the limestone of this cave is cemented, ground up sea shells. Amazing!

I am thinking of this primordial place with its primordial Beings, glowworms, standing as an archetype of primordial vibrations. I feel the ancient vibrations here. They set the stage of thousands and thousands of years ago.

A note: A few years later, I am in Skocjan Cave, Slovenia, another pure, primordial, sacred place on Mother Earth, and here I connect the vibrations of Skocjan Cave to the vibrations of the Glowworm Grotto. The ancient entities associated with Skocjan Cave are very alert and easy to connect with. When I join the vibrations, I 'see' the entities of both places telepathically communicating with each other. They are very excited to have the connection made for them.

Tonight we stay at the THC Waitomo Hotel surrounded by scenery of rural green hills. We are close to the Glowworm Grotto, and our thoughts are on the tiny creatures radiating their luminescent lights in the darkness of the cave. Were they here during the time of Lemuria? Maybe. In any case, their vibrations are pure and strong, vibrations that Mother Earth needs today

During the night, rain begins steadily and quite hard. In the morning it is still raining. Yesterday, when we drove from the airport, we noticed the parched land. Drought! Our waitress last night tells us water is rationed because there was no rain in March, which, I assume, is the month to bring rain. Well, the needed rain has followed us!

This morning we visit the Otorohanga Kiwi House and Native Bird Park, and we are arriving just as the place opens, leaving our wet umbrellas at the entrance in favor of using big umbrellas offered to us. We are walking to the simulated night-time kiwi enclosures set up so kiwis cannot see us, although we can see them. Two large males in separate enclosures are foraging for food near the glass separating us from them. Amazing to see these ancient birds! I am thinking of Lemuria, a time when Man respected Nature. These flightless, night birds would have a chance during the time of Lemuria. I wonder if kiwis existed then.

Later, at the Waitomo Caves Museum, I learn more about the link between ancient times and today. We see a perfect skeleton of a moa, a huge extinct bird of the Dinosaur Age. These were flightless birds native to New Zealand, and the kiwi is regarded as a close relative of the moa.

Near the kiwi exhibit, we look at an ancient lizard of the Dinosaur Age. Other lizards of ancient times are also here. New Zealand is full of surprises! The cook, who is feeding them, says they are fed every two days, and I am wondering if all creatures living in this park are fed every two days.

The bird display throughout the park is impressive. At a pond, home to native water fowl, we see in the center a nesting island. Now we enter a huge netted aviary to see rain forest birds, and later we pick up literature describing the Adopt A Bird program. There are parrots and falcons and other birds here at this park, as one would expect, but attention to detail is outstanding. Not only are the birds explained, but the trees and foliage as well. For example, the resin of a tree on display is used by the Maori to clean their teeth, another is for stopping bleeding, and another is for making weapons, houses, etc.

When we leave this wonderful place of ancient birds and trees, our destination is Marakopa Falls, and we are driving on a mountain road, mindful of its blind curves that need to be carefully maneuvered. We are going along slowly, passing a forest walkway sign to Marakopa Falls, driving steadily toward the coast, and finally the mountains fall away and the road straightens. Ahead are more mountains. We have made a mistake. We are not approaching Marakopa Falls, but instead we arrive at a small outpost called Marakopa, sparsely settled. We are taking an unpaved road to reach a bluff overlooking a beach and the ocean, and here we park our rental car and walk in the rain down the grassy bluff to the black beach of volcanic sand.

We stand in the rain on this black volcanic sand, and for a long time we look out at the powerful blue sea. I can well understand why some live in the small outpost of Marakopa. Then we turn back, walk up the bluff to our waiting car and retrace our way to the sign, Marakopa Falls, we have seen earlier. Here we park, and although the rain has eased, we put on our rain gear. With umbrellas up, we climb down a cliff to walk on a cinder path through a primal rain forest of giant ferns and huge trees draped with long, hanging moss. Wonderful! PRIMAL. PURE. Shades of Lemuria!

The fairies are here! Many, many Nature Spirits, and I am calling in the ancient ones, guardians of this fantastic primal land. To my surprise, a race comes in I do not know. The skin is the color of light charcoal. These here in the ancient rain forest of Marakopa Falls are not Aborigine spirits. They are New Zealand spirits. Very ancient, primitive, yet, sophisticated Beings. AMAZING, all this!

As we walk along, the sound of the falls becomes louder and louder. When we reach the edge of the rain forest, here it is! HUGE. Great amounts of water are rushing over a high cliff. Wonderful to see this! Later, I learn that a mere trickle of water was coming over the cliff until the rain came. Well, the rain is here! Good!!!

We are headed now to Rotorua in Maori country, and we are driving the car toward Hamilton until we reach a sign to Cambridge. Then we turn west to go through rolling hills, sheep and cattle country, the land cleared except in one place that still has heavy, tropical, ancient foliage. When one realizes what was here before the clearing, oh dear! Mother Earth, the people did not think about you when they cleared your land.

We are reaching Route 1, a fast road, and it is raining, sprinkling, raining, sprinkling, some fog. When we reach Route 5, we follow this to Rotorua. The road is clearly marked and we do not have the guessing and uncertainty of two days ago when we struggled to reach the Glowworm Grotto.

Now we arrive at Rotorua and we begin looking for a Maori thermal reserve at the edge of town. Yes, here it is, located in a volcanic area with one of the largest boiling lakes in the world. This is part of the Ring of Fire. I am here to take in the vibrations of this place and to ask the spiritual guardians to remain calm during the coming months of stress.

As we arrive at the reserve, a tour is ready to begin and we join it by climbing aboard a small, yellow, plastic train. A young Maori is guiding us.

Our train glides silently along and I am assuming this is an electric train. Very quickly we reach steaming places in the woods and bushes. Mud pots. And then we are at the continually erupting Pohutu Geyser, actually two geysers that have turned this area into sulfur-laden rocks of varying shades of white and yellow. These geysers are just above a fast-flowing river. One can feel the instability of the place.

With destroying violence, Mount Tarawera has erupted here.

A museum called The Bath House, or, more officially, the City of Rotorua Museum, has an hourly film on the history of this area and we want to see this film. The architecture of this place reminds us of its original intent, a huge, Victorian-style hotel furnished with hot, healing, thermal water piped throughout. We enter to sit in the theater on tiered platforms in front of a large screen.

The film dramatically shows the explosion of Mount Tarawera wrecking everything for miles around. The Maori, says the film, predicted this. During the night of June 9, 1886, the top of Mount Wahanga blew off, followed by Mount Tarawera and Ruawahia exploding with fire. Lava and rocks were thrown 10,000 feet high. The nearby town of Wairoa was covered with ten feet of ash and mud and stone. The noise of the explosions was heard as far away as the South Island of New Zealand.

While the film is showing the violent explosions, the platforms we are sitting on begin to shake and move. Impressive! Interesting how much thought and effort has been put into this program so people will understand the original event.

When the film ends, we visit a Maori spiritual exhibit on the ground floor of the museum, and here we stand in front of a statue of a Maori guardian wearing a flax shirt. He feels alive. At this exhibit is a wall map of part of the Ring of Fire showing the Pacific and Indian Ocean plates coming together and pushing up beneath New Zealand. Another map shows Ring of Fire plates for all of the Pacific.

I am looking at these maps and thinking how important it is for humanity to behave properly in order not to upset Mother Earth. If humanity behaves properly, Mother Earth will protect her children.

It is time now to enjoy a gift from Mother Earth, a healing sulfur bath. At the Rotorua Lakeside Thermal Holiday Park, which will be home for tonight, the owner gives a cautionary comment that the brown stain at the bottom of the tub I am about to use has sulfur stain, not dirt. I am climbing into this big, brown-stained tub of hot, hot water, covering myself with wonderful sulfur water as the tub is filling, and yes, I fill the tub nearly to the top. I lean back, my head barely above the sulfur water, my skin feeling SO GOOD, and I am ENJOYING, ENJOYING, ENJOYING.

━━◆━━

Next day:

The Orchid Gardens at Rotorua is a good place to start the morning. As Margaret and I bring our little rental car to a stop in the parking lot, we see a gardener spraying plants. I am thinking that orchids and other plants love this. A sign says orchids must be watered daily because they cannot hold water.

Inside the building, as I stop to smell a big white orchid with many blossoms, it telepathically tells me that its beauty is to be enjoyed by the sight not by the smell. I pull back, surprised, amused by the unexpected remark, and I answer that I know it had no smell but I wanted to smell it anyway. Another orchid, a small one beside the big white one, says telepathically that I can smell him, and I do.

At 9 a.m. sharp, just past the orchid display, Margaret and I are sitting in a small theater to watch a water organ show, and it is spectacular! As music plays, eight hundred jets of colored water are programmed to spray like dancing nymphs. We watch fascinated! This is a twenty-minute program, and when it finishes, we, the only spectators at this early hour, are asked to return in an hour to see it again.

When we leave the theater, we stop at a small bird display to look at four cockatoos perched together in the only sunshine in their cage. Near the cage is a red pheasant, similar to the one I saw at Mount Koya, Japan. Amazing to see this red pheasant here.

In the afternoon, after our little rental car has taken us here and there, we head for a hot springs town called Miranda with the thought that perhaps a thermal bath may be available this evening. We reach the town of Waitakaruru and head north toward Miranda, but soon the road splits and we do not know which way to turn. We decide to drive toward the water, which we cannot see, but we sense the water. Very quickly we are in swamp land, and it is extensive. There is no town. Where is Miranda? When the road turns away from the swamp, we are relieved and we are driving fast now, wanting to reach Miranda, thinking of a thermal bath. But nothing appears ahead resembling a town.

Now we are approaching a low, modern building set back from the road, and we are bumping along on a dirt road to reach the steps of the building. This place, we learn, is the Miranda Naturalist Trust building, a shore bird center. When we enter, we see bird displays and a man behind a cash register who says when we tell him we are trying to locate Miranda to stay overnight we can stay here. Amazing! He shows us a room with two sets of bunk beds, and we will spend the night on the two lower bunks. Again, amazing! There is no one else here. He lives next door in a house with a yard of machinery, cars, and trucks, and when it is time for him to close the nature center, he locks up and returns to his house.

Margaret and I can get out, though, and we take a walk in a pasture with no cattle or other animals, but a hawk is flying overhead and wild flowers are at our feet. Beyond this pasture are other pastures, the caretaker has told us, and at the far end of these pastures are mango swamps and then water.

Before sunset comes a huge rainbow arching across the dark, rain-threatening sky for miles and miles, descending behind us. We watch this rainbow a long time, its bands heavy with color. Now comes the sunset, and we are seeing bright yellow-orange extensive cloud formations at the horizon. And yes, another rainbow is coming! And so now there are two rainbows side by side. We watch the show nearly an hour, until the colored clouds and rainbows are gone. If we had reached Miranda, we would never have seen such a spectacular sight.

While the rainbows and clouds were entertaining us, we were also watching birds swooping for bugs in a tiny pond just outside the building, this pond lined with tall, stately, white pampas grass. I have been seeing this pampas grass often while driving but I have not stopped to film. Well, I did not film the white pampas grass here! I filmed the two rainbows and the clouds at sunset and I have forgotten the white pampas grass.

When it is dark, we go to bed. Wonderful sleeping here in this quiet place surrounded by Nature. In the night, both of us feel earth tremors.

CHAPTER 11

Fiji

In Chapter 9, on Oshima Island, I mention that it is my understanding that during the ancient time of Lemuria, all fairies living in the Pacific region were programmed to their headquarters located at a waterfall in the jungles of Malaysia. This headquarters still exists, but for whatever reason, perhaps a change in vibration, the fairies long ago forgot their headquarters. Perhaps when the land was inundated with water, the surviving fairies were so disoriented, they clung to whatever piece of land and foliage was available to them, and there they remained. All interchange of activity ceased among fairies. The Fiji fairies knew the Fiji fairies, the Hawaiian fairies knew the Hawaiian fairies, but there was no connection between Cook Island, Fiji Island, Solomon Island fairies, and so forth. As for the headquarters, that concept vanished from their minds. Now it is time to bring the family together by restoring the concept of the headquarters, and so I have begun making connections.

———⟡———

I am in Viti Levu, the main island of Fiji in the South Pacific, and I am riding on Queens Road in a white taxi headed toward the Sleeping Giant Mountain. My driver is Indian, pleasant, patient, his age unknown but probably he is close to forty. We pass a school bus of children ready to enter the airport. My Indian driver tells me these children are from rural Fiji and they are being taken to the airport and to some hotels with modern facilities so they can understand about modern living.

Now he slows our white taxi and pulls off the road to drive on grass near railroad tracks. He is looking for a place where no electric or telephone lines will interfere with my camera lens when I take a photograph of the Sleeping Giant Mountain straight ahead of us. I think he has done this a number of times for tourists. And yes, here is a good place to take a photograph.

Sleeping Giant Mountain is not a tall mountain and it reminds me of Camelback Mountain in Phoenix, except this mountain ahead of me is covered with tropical, green vegetation whereas Camelback is barren. My driver relates the local myth that a giant lay down to rest and then he could not get up. Hence, he is the mountain or vice versa.

I realize the railroad tracks here beside me are for sugar cane. No passenger trains. I see a special type of railroad carrier, open for sugar cane, pulled by an engine. There is much sugar cane activity in Fiji. Are these train carriers busy all year, I ask myself. Trucks laden with cane are coming up the road and I think the cane will be loaded onto train carriers. I have noticed that many cane fields are cut, some in the process of being burned. When I ask why there are so few tropical trees growing wild on Fiji, I am told that they have been destroyed because of constant burning of the sugar cane fields Yes, fields are everywhere, on flat surfaces, on mountain slopes. I am happy Sleeping Giant Mountain, with its thick coat of foliage, has been spared.

Local gossip has already told me that a Colonial (I assume this means an Englishman) wanted to start a big sugar cane business here on Fiji, but the local people would not work for him so he imported indentured Indians who, if they worked a certain length of time, would be allowed to remain on Fiji and have land of their own. Whatever the truth of the matter, many Indians live today in Fiji, and some are owners of flourishing businesses.

Politically, the Indians became strong and ran things until 1987, if my facts are right, when there was a military coup and indigenous people stepped in and declared Fiji a Republic. The British cut Fiji from the Commonwealth, but I note that Fiji money still carries the face of Queen Elizabeth, and so not everything has changed. Many of the 5,000 Indians who fled the island have returned.

My Indian driver is back on the road and we are following the coast until we reach an unpaved road with sugar cane fields on either side. We take this unpaved road and begin to climb a bit, and very quickly we are at the entrance to the Garden of the Sleeping Giant, founded by actor Raymond Burr to be a home for his orchids. He has died, but his garden lives on, and I am told that today this garden has the largest collection of orchids in Fiji.

I leave the taxi to begin walking along a pathway strung with black netting on either side to protect the orchids. And yes, this is a fantastic display of orchids! And yes, the little fairies are here! Fairies everywhere! I am greeting them and speaking to them. This is a bit of Paradise!!!!

I am with the orchids, looking at them, talking to the fairies. I cannot adequately describe how wonderful this place is. After seeing so much earth being abused here in Fiji, so much land without proper vegetation, I am suddenly in Paradise.

I am walking slowly, absorbing, absorbing all this, talking with the fairies, and now I am leaving the orchids and walking in a clipped grass area. I am coming to a pond stuffed with lily pads, and this pond is cut in half by a wooden walkway and a wooden seating area. I am walking slowly on the wooden walkway, walking upward, and now I am hearing a cracking sound like masts on a rolling ship. Ahead of me is a huge clump of tall bamboo swaying in the wind. Yes, the wind has come and the swaying bamboo is making a cracking, cracking noise. Wonderful!

I talk to the wind, remembering the Tor in England where the wind was so strong, it nearly knocked me off the hill, and I had laughed and laughed at my struggle to remain on the hill, talking to the wind trying to knock me off. Or, maybe the wind was trying to get my attention. In any case, from then on, the wind has been my friend.

Everything here in this tropical forest at the Garden of the Sleeping Giant is ALIVE, including the cracking, cracking bamboo, and I am thinking on all of them, talking to all of them here in this Paradise.

Now I turn back to the lily pond to spend a few minutes quietly absorbing everything, reluctant to leave, and then I retrace my steps over the grass to the pathway with the black netting and orchids before walking to a place with overhead faucets turned on to simulate rain, to give the impression of a real tropical garden.

At the main pavilion, I am given a complimentary drink of mango-orange, and I am drinking this, sitting on a high-backed, white, wicker chair that has held a lot of customers over the years. When my drink is finished, I visit a nearby orchid display of small orchids. Beginners, I am thinking. So many small orchids! So many types! Many are bright little yellow orchids.

My Indian driver is waiting to return me to my hotel.

———————

Five years later, I again visit Fiji, and yes, the Sleeping Giant Mountain is the same as earlier, but, the garden? Oh dear. I see few orchids. What has happened? Later, I learn there has been a drought. I know orchids want rain daily, and I am thinking a drought would be exactly what they do not want.

At the Garden of the Sleep Giant, I follow the same path as before, leaving the orchid area, crossing clipped grass, coming to the pond, and I am happy it is still stuffed with lily pads. I walk on the wooden walkway to reach the tall clump of bamboo, and when I reach them, they are silent. No wind today. I miss their cracking noise.

Further up the cliff of bamboo is a seated area, and I am sitting here, taking in the vibrations of this wonderful place. Even though the orchids have fallen on hard times, the fairies are still here, and I am opening to them, talking to them, and they are happy I am here.

I am telling them I am connecting them to their headquarters, this headquarters they have forgotten, and I am using my Light, my energies, my vibrations, to connect them here at Fiji with the headquarters they have forgotten at the waterfall in Malaysia.

I spend time doing this, feeling good about doing this. Yes, connecting the little ones to their headquarters is a feeling-good task, and I am sitting here a long time before retracing my steps, passing the tall bamboo, the pond, the grassy area, the few orchids. I am spending a bit of time at the pavilion before getting into my taxi to return to my hotel.

A friend is sharing the taxi with me, and as we are driving away from the garden, she turns to look back. She tells me to look back. I turn my head, and there, at the place where the little fairies of the Garden of the Sleeping Giant have been connected to their headquarters in Malaysia, I see bright lines of Light/energy coming down from the sky. Ten, twelve lines. AMAZING!

Another reason why I have come to the Pacific is to help weave a tapestry of energy to mend a break in the aura of Mother Earth created when humanity made an artificial time line running north and south in the Pacific, so that at a specific place, one calendar day becomes the next day.

On this journey, I fly from Los Angeles across the artificial line to Fiji, then Fiji across the line to Samoa, then Samoa across the line to New Zealand, and finally across the artificial line to the USA. When I leave Fiji, I sit at a plane window next to an older, kind Samoan woman, her Polynesian face wide. She is wearing over her heavy body a typical Polynesian-style dress, faded red/white floral. She tells me she is widowed, her husband having had a stroke and dying within three weeks of the beginning of his illness. She has taught eighteen years in Fiji before working for the government. She lives alone and she is flying today to live for a time with her family in Samoa. Probably, she says, she will stay four weeks, then fly back to Fiji, and then to Australia where she has a child. She goes back and forth among family members.

As we are talking, the pilot announces that we are flying across the International Date Line and I joke with her about this and ask what does she think of this abrupt change from April 3, Tuesday, in Fiji to April 2, Monday, in Samoa. She shrugs her shoulders and says it is silly. I am thinking about this artificial time line set up half a world away in Greenwich during the British domination of the waters and islands of the Pacific. Those who set up this time system have not asked the islanders what they think. If there are consequences, then the islanders must live with them.

As I am thinking about this artificial time line, I am looking out the plane window at the blue Pacific. Below me, white clouds are lined up like soldiers, east to west, according to how the wind has lined them up.

CHAPTER 12

Removing Excess Energy
from The Ring of Fire

January 3, 2008:

I am tracking down Kathleen who lives in the USA, and I speak to her by phone at 11:30 a.m. I tell her that the Ring of Fire is ready to blow in a serious manner. She replies that she is very ill. She has terrible arthritis over her entire body and she is in constant pain. Her voice sounds weak but I note there is some spunk left in her. I tell her she is needed, and I am asking her to look at the volcanoes in Indonesia. She looks and says there is too much build up of energy. Yes, I am agreeing, and I tell her to pull the excess energy out of Indonesia and send it to Pele, goddess head of the Pacific, she at the center of the Ring of Fire, Hawaii, also center of ancient Lemuria.

Kathleen is pulling out the excess energy and I am seeing it going to Pele. Good!

She comments that the tone of the Indonesian energy is high notes, like coming from a violin. Yes, I can hear them. Now she is going to Japan and taking out excess energy and sending it to Pele. This sound, she says, is low, like a base tone. I am hearing them. Now she is going to the Russian peninsula and taking out excess energy and sending it to Pele and her comment is that the sound is like sharp bells. Yes. I can hear them. I can hear all the sounds of the excess energy that Kathleen is sending to Pele. I ask her to take excess energy off the Aleutian Range of Alaska, and she is doing this. I ask her to look at California, which I see does not have a problem today, and she is looking and agreeing that there is no problem. Check Mexico, I tell her, and she is looking at Mount Popocatepetl with the smoke coming out a bit but there is no particular problem here. We are looking at Mexico in the North and there are two volcano places. The one I know well is okay, but the other, the new one, as Kathleen labels this place, has too much energy and so she is sending some to Pele.

I ask her to check near Lima, Peru but she does not know the place, and I am telling her the area is okay. Check Chile, I tell her, and she says she has never been to Chile, but she has been to Cuzco, Peru. I tell her to follow my mind inland from Cuzco and she will come to a Chilean volcano where I have taken excess energy off and handed it to Pele. Then I check the spine of South America called Andes Mountains and I am telling her there is too much energy up and down that mountain range. Together, we pull excess energy off that place and send it to Pele. Now I tell her to look briefly at Antarctica and take some off there, this place having active volcanoes, and then I tell her to take excess energy off New Zealand, this place always a potential risk.

Kathleen and I have been circling the Ring of Fire to take off excess energy and we have been giving it to Pele.

It is coming close to 12 noon, time to meditate. Pele is ready, baton in hand, to begin conducting the orchestra of sounds/instruments/excess energy from the Ring of Fire. But what is the music? She needs to use her baton to conduct the orchestra for playing music. The excess energy must be turned into music.

I begin playing a CD called Let There Be Peace On Earth, and I hear a beautiful Japanese female voice singing this beautiful song.

Pele is now conducting the orchestra of excess energy.

EXCESS ENERGY IS BEING TURNED INTO MUSIC for all of Mother Earth, to take away her belly ache at the Ring of Fire.

LET THERE BE PEACE ON EARTH. That is the music.

Create, create, create, create to correct the excess energy. That is how it is done.

I want this book to end with a footnote:

A few years ago, when I was waking, I suddenly had a vivid picture, like a movie, of people wearing white coats, lying on their backs, floating down a wide, wide river or expanse of water. It was the dead of winter.

All floating on the water were dead.

People were standing in the snow next to the edge of the wide expanse of water, but they had no boats or any means of rescuing the floating dead.

My first thought was Siberia. This action is taking place in Siberia.

I was busy during the morning and I did not think about what I had seen. Yet, it remained in the back of my mind until just before 12 noon and I suddenly knew I must phone Kathleen to tell her. I phoned and she answered immediately. She listened to my brief story without interruption and when I finished, she asked what was the color of the coats the dead people were wearing. White.

We both knew the answer: Siberia! Kamchatka Peninsula!

Excess energy was POWERFUL at the plates off the peninsula. It needed to be removed!

And yes, we removed the excess energy.

Then we spoke again, and we both agreed that we had less than a half hour before the plates moved and a tsunami would have brought the water to the Kamchatka Peninsula and killed the people.

Later, I asked the Higher Worlds why I was shown such a gruesome scene when it did not happen. The answer came quickly. If we had not acted immediately, the scene would have been true.

And so, readers, remember, nothing happens until it happens. Create the positive to discourage the negative.